“Computer Viruses Unveiled: Types, Trends and Mitigation Strategies”

GoodMan, Volume 1

Patrick Mukosha

Published by Patrick Mukosha, 2023.

Also by Patrick Mukosha

GoodMan

Resilient Strategies: Thriving in Harsh Business Conditions
Strategic Entrepreneurship: Navigating The Path To Success
Decisive Power: Navigating How to Make Toughest Decisions
Unraveling Information Systems: Exploring the Core Concepts
"Reigning the Boardroom: A Trailblazing Guide to Corporate Governance Success"
Fortifying Digital Fortress: A Comprehensive Guide to Information Systems Security
"Unleashing the Power of Inclusive Innovation: Transforming the World for All"
"Exploring Computer Systems: From Fundamentals to Advanced Concepts"
"Computer Viruses Unveiled: Types, Trends and Mitigation Strategies"

Dedication

The author is indebted to a large number of researchers, and consultants in the field of Information and Communication Technologies (ICT), whose works were referred to in writing this book – and appears below and in the bibliography.

The author also would like to acknowledge the encouragement of my wife; Gracious Lumba Maboshe-Mukosha, my special colleagues Bernard Chisanga (MHSRIP), and Amos Wambili, and my children, whose comments and constructive criticism kept the author alive. The author also benefitted from the comments of many colleagues: Paul Wilson and Peter Bird. They generously shared their insights and experiences in an evolving field where tacit knowledge is indispensable.

The author wishes to thank his late Father; Isaac Mulando Mukosha (MHSRIP) and late mother; Rebecca Mukosha (MHSRIP), for their endless love. This book has been dedicated to my young sister, Loveness Mukosha (MHSRIP). She worked tirelessly to improve her academic education, and achieved a lot at a tender age.

Special thanks go to Lionel Hugh Weston; my former Secondary School Teacher and Guardian, without whom I would never have had a strong education foundation in life. His contribution in my education career is immeasurable. I shall forever remain indebted to him and the entire Weston's family.

"Title: Computer Viruses Unveiled: *Types, Trends and Mitigation Strategies*"

Copyright Notice

First published: August, 2023

Publisher: Patrick Mukosha PhD

Trademarks

All terms mentioned in this book that are known to be trademarks or service marks have been appropriately capitalized. The Author and the publisher cannot attest to the accuracy of this information. Use of a term in this book should not be regarded as affecting the validity of any trademark or service mark.

Warning and Disclaimer

Every effort has been made to make this book as complete and as accurate as possible, but no warranty or fitness is implied. The information provided in this book is on as is basis. The Author and the Publisher shall have neither liability nor responsibility to any person or entity with respect to any loss or damage arising from the use the information contained in this book.

Author: Patrick Chisenga Mukosha PhD

Abstract

In the digital age, where information technology is integral to our daily lives, the threat of computer viruses looms ever larger. "Computer Viruses Unveiled: Types, Trends, and Mitigation Strategies" is a comprehensive guide that explores the complex world of computer viruses, shedding light on their types, evolving trends, and effective mitigation strategies.

"Computer Viruses Unveiled" meticulously categorizes various types of computer viruses, from classic boot sector viruses to modern ransomware and advanced persistent threats (APTs).

One of the book's standout features is its exploration of the ever-changing landscape of computer viruses. It discusses emerging trends in cyber threats, such as fileless malware and zero-day exploits, offering insights into how hackers continually adapt their tactics to infiltrate systems. It covers essential topics like antivirus software, intrusion detection systems, and network segmentation. Moreover, it emphasizes the role of user education and security awareness programs in preventing infections.

"Computer Viruses Unveiled" addresses the future of cybersecurity. It discusses the impact of emerging technologies like artificial intelligence and quantum computing on both the offensive and defensive aspects of computer virus warfare. It challenges readers to think about the ethical and moral implications of these technologies in the context of cybersecurity.

This book is ideal for a wide audience, including IT professionals, cybersecurity enthusiasts, business leaders, and anyone interested in safeguarding their digital assets. It's written in a clear and accessible manner, making it suitable for both technical and non-technical readers.

"Computer Viruses Unveiled: Types, Trends, and Mitigation Strategies" is an indispensable resource for anyone looking to navigate the intricate world of computer viruses and protect their digital world from the ever-present threat of cyberattacks.

1. Introduction: The Evolving Threat Landscape

The ever-developing threats and difficulties that people, companies, and society encounter in the context of cybersecurity and elsewhere are referred to as the "evolving threat landscape." Due to technical breakthroughs, fluctuating geopolitical factors, and the inventiveness of threat actors, this terrain is constantly changing.

The following are some crucial elements of the changing threat landscape:

a. **Cybersecurity Threats:** The sophistication and scope of cyberattacks continue to increase. Threat actors might be nation-states, organized cybercrime groups, individual hackers, or hacktivists. Malware, ransomware, phishing, and distributed denial-of-service (DDoS) attacks are examples of common cyber threats.
b. **Advanced Persistent Threats (APTs):** Nation-states or well-funded organizations frequently launch these persistent, targeted cyberattacks. They seek to espionage or otherwise enter a target network and remain unnoticed there for an extended period of time.
c. **IoT and OT Vulnerabilities:** The attack surface has increased as a result of the proliferation of Internet of Things (IoT) devices and the integration of operational technology (OT) and information technology (IT). Cybercriminals may use insecure IoT and OT devices to obtain illegal access or disable vital infrastructure.
d. **Cloud Security:** As businesses move their data and services to the cloud more frequently, cloud security is becoming a major worry. Risks associated with configuration errors, weak access controls, and data breaches in cloud systems are substantial.

e. **Attacks on the Supply Chain:** Attackers are now concentrating on finding weaknesses in the supply chain. Compromising hardware, software updates, or outside vendors might have serious repercussions.
f. **Artificial Intelligence (AI) and Machine Learning (ML):** Both security experts and bad actors are using AI and ML. However, they can also be used to automate attacks and create more convincing phishing emails. AI-powered technologies can improve cybersecurity defences.
g. **Edge computing and 5G:** The use of edge computing and the rollout of 5G networks provide new security problems. The attack surface and possible vulnerabilities are increased by these technologies, which also make data processing faster.
h. **Privacy Issues and Regulatory Compliance:** Organizations must have strong data security measures in place in order to comply with data protection laws like GDPR and CCPA. Heavy fines and reputational harm might come from noncompliance.
i. **Geopolitical Factors:** Nation-states may engage in cyber-espionage, cyberwarfare, and misinformation campaigns as a result of geopolitical conflicts.
j. **Human Component**: Despite technology breakthroughs, people continue to be a cybersecurity weak link. Attacks that use social engineering to influence people's behaviour, like phishing, are common.
k. **Emerging Technologies:** Cutting-edge innovations like blockchain and quantum computing pose both opportunities and risks. While blockchain can potentially improve security in some use cases, quantum computing has the potential to compromise present encryption techniques.
l. **Environmental Issues:** Natural catastrophes and climate change can affect the accessibility and reliability of digital

infrastructure, creating security risks.

Organizations must develop a proactive and adaptive approach to cybersecurity in response to the changing threat landscape. Strong security rules, frequent vulnerability assessments, employee training, incident response plans, and cooperation with law enforcement and cybersecurity professionals are all part of this. To effectively manage risks, it is also crucial to be educated about new security threats and to make investments in cutting-edge security technologies.

2. The Importance of Cybersecurity

In the linked, digital world of today, cybersecurity is of the utmost significance. Its importance spans numerous industries, from people and small businesses to huge corporations, governments, and providers of essential infrastructure.

Here are some major justifications for why cybersecurity is crucial:

a. **Protection of Data and Privacy:** Sensitive data is stored online by both individuals and corporations, and it is a valuable asset. Cybersecurity guards against theft, unauthorized access, and breaches so that people's privacy and trust are upheld.
b. **Financial Loss Prevention**: Cyberattacks can cause large financial losses. Financial fraud and identity theft, for instance, can empty people's bank accounts and harm businesses while ransomware attacks have the potential to result in the extortion of significant quantities of money.
c. **Reputation Protection:** A cyberattack can seriously harm an organization's reputation. People frequently stop trusting organizations that can't protect their data. After a breach, re-establishing confidence can be difficult and expensive.
d. **Keeping Operations Running:** Data breaches and distributed denial-of-service (DDoS) attacks can disrupt business operations and cause downtime. A strong cybersecurity strategy reduces interruptions and supports business continuity.
e. **Protection of Intellectual Property**: For a competitive advantage, many firms rely on their intellectual property. Trade secrets, research, and development efforts are shielded from theft and industrial espionage by cybersecurity measures.
f. **National Security:** To safeguard sensitive data, military

systems, and essential infrastructure, governments and nation-states have a vested interest in cybersecurity. Geopolitically significant ramifications can result from cyberattacks.

g. **Compliance and Legal Obligations**: To safeguard customer data and privacy, regulatory authorities establish cybersecurity standards. Non-compliance may have negative legal repercussions, penalties, and obligations.
h. **Human Safety:** Cyberattacks occasionally put the general public's safety at risk. This covers assaults on the emergency services, transportation networks, and healthcare systems. To protect lives of people, it is essential to ensure the security of these systems.
i. **Security in The Supply Chain:** As supply chains grow more interconnected, cybersecurity is crucial to guaranteeing the quality of goods and services. Attacks on the supply chain may have far-reaching repercussions.
j. **Threat environment Evolution:** As hackers become more skilled and inventive, the threat environment is constantly changing. To protect against ever-evolving threats, organizations must adapt and increase their cybersecurity procedures.
k. **Internet of Things (IoT) Security**: As IoT devices proliferate, new security issues arise. IoT devices that are not secure can be used to conduct attacks or break into networks. To protect against these dangers, appropriate cybersecurity measures are essential.
l. **Global Connectivity**: Because the world's economies and digital systems are interconnected, a cyberattack in one region of the world can have repercussions throughout the entire planet. This emphasizes the importance of multinational collaboration in cybersecurity initiatives.
m. **Protection of Democracy:** The democratic process is in

danger due to cyberattacks that try to sabotage elections and disseminate false information. The credibility of elections and democratic institutions depends on strong cybersecurity.

Therefore, cybersecurity is an essential component of contemporary life and business, not only a technical issue. Individuals, organizations, and governments are more susceptible to cyber dangers as a result of the growing reliance on digital technology. Protecting privacy, security, and the ongoing operation of our interconnected world require an understanding of the importance of cybersecurity and the adoption of preventative steps to defend against these threats.

Chapter 1: Understanding Computer Viruses

1.1. What Are Computer Viruses?

A specific kind of malware called a computer virus multiplies itself after being run by altering other software and injecting its own code. The damaged areas are then referred to as being "infected" with a computer virus, a metaphor borrowed from biological viruses, if this replication is successful.

A host software is typically necessary for computer infections. The host program is infected with the virus's own code. The written virus program is performed first when the program is run, infecting and harming the system. A computer worm, on the other hand, doesn't require a host application because it is a standalone piece of code. As a result, it is not constrained by the host application and is free to operate independently and engage in active attack activity.

To initially infect systems and disseminate the virus, virus writers use social engineering ruses and exploit in-depth knowledge of security weaknesses. To avoid detection by antivirus software, viruses employ sophisticated anti-detection/stealth techniques. Some of the reasons people create viruses are to make money (such as with ransomware), to send a message, for personal amusement, to show that a software vulnerability exists, for sabotage and denial of service, or just to investigate cybersecurity issues, artificial life, and evolutionary algorithms.

Computer viruses are nefarious software applications created with the intention of infecting, replicating, and spreading to other computers and systems. Because of their capacity to multiply and "infect" other software or files, they constitute a subset of malware (malicious software) and were given the term of biological viruses.

The following are the main traits and elements of computer viruses:

1.1.1. **Replication:** Viruses are designed to reproduce and spread to more computers, applications, or files. They accomplish this by "infecting" a host file or program by attaching their code to it.

1.1.2. **Destructive and Malicious Intent:** Computer viruses, as opposed to benign or harmless software, have destructive or malicious intentions. They are capable of carrying out a variety of hazardous tasks, including as altering data, stealing information, or causing harm to the infected machine.

1.1.3. **Hidden Execution**: Viruses frequently hide within what appear to be trustworthy files or programs. When a user runs, opens, or accesses an infected file or program, the viral code is turned on and begins to do its evil things.

1.1.4. **Payload:** A virus usually carries a payload, which is the malicious function that it is designed to carry out. This payload can do a broad range of things, from displaying obnoxious messages to erasing files, stealing data, or even converting an infected computer into a botnet for use in cybercrime.

1.1.5. **Propagation:** Computer viruses have ways to get into other systems and spread there. This can happen in a number of ways, including contaminated software downloads, removable storage devices, infected email attachments, and exploiting weaknesses in the target system.

1.1.6. **Concealment:** Viruses frequently adopt methods to hide their presence in order to avoid being found and eliminated. This includes techniques to change their code, elude detection by antivirus software, or conceal themselves in system files.

1.1.7. **Activation Trigger:** Some viruses are engineered to only execute when certain circumstances or triggers are met, such as a set date or the presence of a specific file on the infected system.

1.1.8. **Self-Modification**: In order to evade detection by antivirus software that relies on signatures, viruses may regularly alter their code. This makes them more difficult to find and get rid of.

Not every bad software is officially a virus, despite the fact that the term "virus" is frequently used to describe a range of destructive programs. Worms, Trojans, spyware, adware, and ransomware are some other forms of malware, each having unique traits and methods of operation. Within the larger category of malware, viruses are but one subset. Utilizing antivirus and antimalware software, updating operating systems and software with security patches, following safe computing practices (such as not downloading files from unknown sources or opening suspicious email attachments), and regularly backing up important data are all part of protecting against computer viruses and other malware.

1.2. A Brief History of Computer Viruses

The history of computer viruses spans several decades and has changed as computers and the internet have advanced. Here is a quick rundown of significant turning points in the history of computer viruses:

1.2.1. **1940s–1970s Early Experiments**: In academic and experimental settings, the idea of self-replicating programs—a forerunner to computer viruses—was investigated as early as the 1940s. Researchers created self-replicating programs that weren't malevolent in nature throughout the 1960s and 1970s. The primary focus of these early efforts was academic.

1.2.2. **The First Computer Virus (1970s):** Fred Cohen, a computer scientist, first used the term "computer virus" in 1983. However, Bob Thomas developed the "Creeper" virus, the first real computer virus, in the early 1970s. Creeper corrupted the PDP-10 mainframe computers of Digital Equipment Corporation (DEC), displaying the message "I'm the creeper, catch me if you can!"

1.2.3. **1980s: The First Antivirus Program:** Ray Tomlinson developed the first antivirus program, termed "Reaper," in 1971 in response to the Creeper virus and following threats. Reaper was created to get rid of the Creeper infection from compromised computers.

1.2.4. **The Development of Computer Viruses (1980s–1990s):** Viruses that target personal computers were increasingly common in the 1980s. Many people believe that the "Brain" virus, which initially appeared in 1986, was the first PC infection. It altered the boot sector of the disk and propagated via contaminated floppy disks. One of the first viruses to employ stealth tactics to avoid detection was the "Vienna" virus in 1987. PC viruses increased dramatically in the late 1980s and early 1990s, including the notorious "Michelangelo" virus that, on Michelangelo's birthday, raised concerns about widespread data destruction.

1.2.5. **Internet spread of worms in the 1990s:** Worms began to appear in the 1990s, including the "Morris Worm" in 1988, which spread throughout the early internet and significantly disrupted operations. In 2000, the "ILOVEYOU" worm, one of the most pervasive and harmful malware attacks at the time, spread via email and resulted in enormous financial losses.

1.2.6. **Modern Period (Since the 2000s):** The rapid evolution of malware in the twenty-first century included the emergence of complex Trojans, spyware, ransomware, and state-sponsored cyberattacks. A noteworthy example of state-sponsored malware created to obstruct Iran's nuclear development is Stuxnet, which was found in 2010. Because of their extensive effects, ransomware attacks like WannaCry (2017) and NotPetya (2017) have drawn attention from all across the world.

Cybercriminals continue to use more sophisticated methods and new weaknesses to further the evolution of malware. To identify and lessen the effects of computer viruses and other types of malware during the course of this history, the cybersecurity sector has created antivirus and security software. However, the continual cat-and-mouse game between malware developers and cybersecurity experts underscores the significance of cybersecurity policies and safeguards.

1.3. Types of Viruses: Malware, Ransomware, Trojans, Worms, and More

Computer code that is malevolent is referred to as malware. As previously stated, a virus is a special type of malware that infects other programs and can only function when those programs are running. Malware that can operate, reproduce, and spread on its own is known as a worm, and malware that deceives users into launching it by posing as a helpful program or document is known as a Trojan horse. A subset of malware are computer viruses, and there are many other kinds and classifications of malware.

The most typical malware, which includes viruses, ransomware, Trojans, worms, and more, are listed below:

1.3.1. **Computer Viruses:** Computer viruses, as was previously said, are self-replicating programs that affix themselves to trustworthy files or applications. When the infected software is run, they can carry out evil deeds and propagate by contaminating other files.

1.3.2. **Ransomware:** A form of virus known as ransomware locks the victim out of their own computer system or encrypts their contents. In order to unlock the files or regain access to the machine, attackers demand a ransom, typically in bitcoin.

1.3.3. **Trojan Horses (Trojans):** Trojans are forms of malware that pose as trustworthy or good-natured programs while actually harbouring dangerous code. Although they don't replicate themselves like viruses do, they frequently act as a backdoor for attackers to access a victim's machine without authorization.

1.3.4. **Worms:** A host file is not required for the self-replicating malware known as worms to spread across networks and computer systems. They can disrupt and congest networks by infecting other machines by taking advantage of weaknesses.

1.3.5. **Spyware:** Spyware is made to stealthily observe a user's computer usage. It has the ability to intercept private data, including keystrokes, passwords, and browsing history, and deliver it to nefarious parties.

1.3.6. **Adware:** Adware can be unpleasant but is often not as malicious as other forms of malware. To make money for its developers, it shows too many unwelcome advertising. Adware may occasionally monitor user behaviour.

1.3.7. **Keyloggers:** A kind of spyware known as Keyloggers records keystrokes made on a victim's PC or mobile device. They have the ability to record private chats, credit card numbers, and other sensitive data.

1.3.8. **Botnets:** Networks of hijacked computers known as botnets are frequently managed remotely by cybercriminals. These "bots" can be employed for a number of harmful activities, such as DDoS attacks, spam distribution, and cryptocurrency mining.

1.3.9. **Rootkits:** Malware called rootkits seeks to take over a machine or network at the administrative level. They are frequently used to keep an infected machine open and conceal the presence of further malware.

1.3.10. **Fileless Malware:** Malware that lacks executable files does not use common executable files. Instead, it is stored in the memory of a computer, making it more difficult to find and get rid of. It has the ability to engage in malicious activity by utilizing reputable system tools and processes.

1.3.11. **Drive-by Downloads**: Drive-by downloads happen when a user visits a hacked or malicious website and unwittingly downloads malware. The majority of the time, browser flaws are used to spread the infection.

1.3.12. **Mobile Malware:** Mobile devices are also impacted by malware. There are many different varieties of mobile malware, including mobile viruses, spyware, and fraudulent apps that aim to infiltrate cell phones.

1.3.13. **Remote Access Trojans (RATs):** RATs give hackers remote access to a victim's computer. They can be employed for a variety of nefarious activities, such as data stealing, monitoring, and initiating assaults on other systems.

1.3.14. **Cryptojacking:** Cryptojacking software uses the processing power of the victim's computer or mobile device to mine bitcoins for the attacker, frequently slowing down the victim's device in the process.

1.3.15. **File Encryptors:** File Encryptors encrypt a user's files without requesting a ransom, similar to ransomware. They might simply erase the data or make them permanently inaccessible.

For individuals and companies to implement successful cybersecurity measures, such as powerful antivirus software, regular software updates, user education, and best practices for safe online conduct, they must have a thorough understanding of these many types of malware.

1.3.16. **Signs of a Computer Virus:** The code used by malware writers is invisible until the payload is delivered. While the virus is active, however, faults, like any software program, could cause problems. You can tell if you have a computer virus by:

- The computer frequently freezes, runs out of memory with only a few open apps, or displays the Windows blue screen of death.
- Adware-containing pop-up windows with advertisements or connections to dangerous websites.
- Without your awareness or involvement with the account, passwords can change.
- Error messages frequently appear when performing simple tasks like opening or using programs.
- Your web browser's home page changes without your intervention.
- You are notified of unusual communications sent by your account via outgoing emails to the persons on your contact list or people you have added to it.
- Even when only a few programs are open or the computer has just been launched, it runs slowly.
- Whenever the computer boots or whenever you activate it, unknown programs.

1.4. How Viruses Infect Systems

Computer systems are infected by viruses using a variety of techniques and mechanisms. Depending on the type of virus and how it was created, different infection techniques may be used. Here are a few typical methods that viruses infiltrate computers:

1.4.1. **Infected Software or Files**: Numerous malware integrate with trustworthy files or software applications. The virus code is executed and the system is infected when a user starts or opens the infected file or software. This is a typical technique employed by viruses to infect files.

1.4.2. **Attachments to Emails:** A popular method for spreading viruses is via email. Email attachments can include viruses, which frequently take the form of executable files or documents containing malicious macros. The virus is launched when the receiver opens the attachment.

1.4.3. **Malicious Downloads:** Users may unintentionally download malware from rogue websites or genuine websites that have been infiltrated. When a person visits a compromised website, malware is instantly downloaded to their computer via a drive-by download.

1.4.4. **Removable Media:** Removable storage devices including USB drives, external hard drives, and SD cards can propagate viruses. The virus may start running automatically or urge the user to open infected files when a storage device that is infected is connected to a computer.

1.4.5. **Network Vulnerabilities:** To spread across linked computers, worms and other network-based infections take advantage of holes in network protocols and services. They frequently search out and attack weak systems in a network.

1.4.6. **Social Engineering:** Some viruses lure people into running them by using social engineering techniques. For instance, a virus may pose as an alluring download and pretend to be a free program or game in order to trick consumers into installing it.

1.4.7. **Exploiting Software Vulnerability**: Software flaws, often known as exploits, can be used by viruses to gain access to a system. Users leave their systems open to these kinds of attacks when they neglect to implement security patches and upgrades.

1.4.8. **Phishing and Negative Connections:** Links to bogus websites harbouring dangerous code are a common feature of phishing emails. Users that connect with the phony website by clicking on these links could unintentionally download infections.

1.4.9. **Apps for Social Media and Messaging**: Through social media sites, messaging services, and peer-to-peer networks, some viruses and malware spread. Users may fall for their tricks and click on fraudulent websites or download harmful files.

1.4.10. **Software Bundling**: It is possible for viruses to be downloaded together with ostensibly reliable applications. Users who download and install such applications run the risk of unintentionally infecting their systems with viruses.

1.4.11. **Torrents and File Sharing**: Viruses can occasionally be found in files exchanged over peer-to-peer (P2P), torrent, or file-sharing services. When users download and open these files, their systems could become infected.

1.4.12. **AutoRun Function**: Some viruses take advantage of the Windows operating system's AutoRun feature, which runs applications from attached removable media automatically. This can cause the infection to start up automatically.

1.4.13. **Social Engineering Attacks**: Social engineering techniques like phishing emails or misleading pop-up messages that entice users to download malicious software or click on links can be used to spread viruses.

1.4.14. Table Summarizing Different Types Of Viruses, How They Attack Computer Systems, And The Best Mitigation Strategies For Each Type:

S/N	Type of Virus	Attack Method	Mitigation Strategies
1	**Malware**	Malware encompasses various types:	- Use reputable antivirus software and keep it updated.
		Trojans: Deceptive software that appears legitimate but contains malicious code.	- Regularly scan your system for malware. - Be cautious when downloading and opening attachments.
		Viruses: Self-replicating code that attaches to legitimate programs.	- Avoid clicking on suspicious links and websites.
2	**Ransomware**	Encrypts user files and demands a ransom for decryption.	Regularly back up data offline Be cautious with email attachments and links. Keep systems and software up to date.
3	**Worms**	Self-replicating malware that spreads across networks without user intervention.	Use a firewall to block suspicious network traffic Isolate infected systems to prevent spreading Patch system vulnerabilities

			promptly
4	**Spyware**	Secretly collects user information, including keystrokes, without user consent.	Use anti-spyware software. Be cautious when downloading freeware or shareware Regularly review browser extensions and plugins.
5	**Adware**	Displays unwanted advertisements, often bundled with free software.	Use ad-blockers or browser extensions. Be cautious when downloading freeware or shareware.
6	**Keyloggers**	Records keystrokes to steal sensitive information, such as passwords.	Use anti-Keyloggers software.
			Be cautious when installing software from untrusted sources.
7	**Rootkit**	Conceals malicious activities by compromising system-level functions.	Use intrusion detection and prevention systems Regularly scan systems for rootkits.
8	**Botnet**	Infects computers to form a network of controlled "bots" for malicious purposes (e.g.,	Use network intrusion detection systems

		DDoS attacks).	Keep systems updated and patched Implement strong network access controls
9	**Fileless Malware**	Operates in memory without leaving traces on disk, making it difficult to detect.	Regularly update and patch software and systems Use advanced endpoint detection and response (EDR) solutions.

Figure 1: Table Summarizing Different Types of Viruses, How They Attack Computer Systems, And the Best Mitigation Strategies for Each Type

Note: The effectiveness of mitigation strategies can vary, and it's essential to adopt a multi-layered approach to cybersecurity, combining security tools, user awareness, and best practices to protect against various types of viruses and malware. Additionally, regularly updating systems and software is crucial in mitigating vulnerabilities that could be exploited by different types of malware.

A virus can carry out its harmful intentions once it has successfully infected a system. These malicious intentions may include stealing information, corrupting data, propagating to other computers, or acting as a backdoor for remote attackers. Strong cybersecurity policies, maintaining software updates, using reliable antivirus software, and educating users about the dangers of downloading and running unknown files or clicking on dubious links are all things that people and organizations can do to prevent virus infestations.

1.4.15: **Virus Removal Instructions**

Although getting rid of a computer infection can be difficult, there are various actions you can take. Typical procedures for removing a computer infection include:

- **Scan For Viruses**: Use your antivirus program to do a full scan, using the most exhaustive or comprehensive option. Cover all of your hard drive letters if you can throughout the scan.
- **Download And Install Antivirus Software**: If possible, download and install a real-time and on-demand antivirus solution if you don't already have it. While you use the computer, a real-time malware scanner checks for infections in the background. Every time you wish to scan your device, you must first launch the on-demand scanner.
- **Delete Or Quarantine The Virus:** Your antivirus program will give you the choice to quarantine or delete the infection once it has been identified. To stop the virus from doing more harm, quarantining it will separate it from the rest of your computer.
- **Delete Any Temporary Files:** Depending on the virus, some viruses are made to start when your computer boots up; therefore, eliminating temporary files may also remove the virus.
- **Disconnect From The Internet:** Because certain computer viruses rely on an internet connection to spread, it's best to do so when eradicating one from your PC in order to avoid additional harm.
- **Reboot your Computer into Safe Mode**: In order to lessen damage to your computer while eradicating a virus, restart your device in "Safe Mode." This will stop the virus from spreading and make it easier for you to get rid of it.
- **Restart Your Computer:** You can restart your computer if

you've successfully eradicated the infection. Simply switch on the device as you normally would, skipping the "Safe Mode" menu.

- **Update Your Operating System And Web Browser To The Most Recent Versions:** To finish the malware removal procedure, update your operating system and web browser to the most recent versions available. Updates for the OS and browser frequently include patches for specific flaws and exploits.

Given that this procedure is broad, the results may differ from virus to virus and from device to device. If you're unsure whether you've successfully eliminated a virus from your computer, seek assistance from an IT or computer expert.

1.4.16: **Computer Virus Prevention Techniques**

Computer viruses can harm your PC, leak private information to hackers, and prevent use of the system while repairs are being made. By adhering to a few basic practices, you can prevent being the next victim of a computer virus:

- **Install Antivirus Software**: Any device linked to the network should be running antivirus software. Your first line of protection against viruses is it. Malware executables are prevented from launching on your local device by antivirus software.
- **Use Only Legal Software**: Although it may be alluring, free pirated software frequently comes bundled with malware. Avoid utilizing shared or pirated software and only download from the vendor's official website.
- **Avoid Opening Executable Email Attachments:** A malicious email attachment is the first step in many malware assaults, including ransomware. Users should avoid running macros coded into files like Microsoft Word or Excel and

should never open executable attachments.

- **Update Your Operating System:** Patches are released by developers for all major operating systems to fix common bugs and security issues. Avoid utilizing out-of-date operating systems, such as old versions of software, and always keep your operating system updated.
- **Utilize Secure Passwords**: Ensure that your passwords are both highly secure and challenging to crack. To reduce weaknesses and stop thieves from stealing, avoid using the same password on several accounts and change it frequently.
- **Stay Away From Dubious Websites:** An exploit can be utilized when just browsing a webpage on older browsers. To avoid drive-by downloads or being redirected to websites that host malware, you should always keep your browser updated with the most recent updates and stay away from these websites.
- **Keep An Eye Out:** Be careful whenever downloading software or files from the internet or opening dubious email attachments. Never give someone you don't know access to your computer; turn off file sharing. Additionally, refrain from storing confidential or delicate information on your computer.

1.14.17: **Examples Of Computers Viruses:** There are millions of computer viruses on the internet, but only a select few have become well-known and infect a staggering number of computers. Typical examples of computer viruses are as follows:

- **Shlayer:** Is a Trojan designed specifically for macOS that spreads mostly through bogus software updates and downloads, bringing adware.
- **Conficker:** This worm, which first appeared in 2008, took use of flaws in Windows operating systems to build a sizable

botnet and infect many users.

- **Morris Worm:** One of the first and most well-known examples of a computer virus, swept via the early Internet in 1988 and caused many computers to slow down or crash.
- **ILOVEYOU**: Was a very damaging worm that overwrote files and spread over email while posing as a declaration of love in 2000.
- **Stuxnet**: Was an advanced worm created in 2010 to target and compromise industrial control systems, especially Iran's nuclear program, by taking advantage of zero-day vulnerabilities.
- **CryptoLocker**: In 2013, the ransomware Trojan CryptoLocker infected hundreds of thousands of PCs and demanded payment to decrypt the victims' contents.
- **Tinba**: Is a banking Trojan that was first identified in 2012, primarily targeted financial institutions with the intention of stealing account details and login passwords.
- **Nimda Worm:** In 2001, the Nimda worm, which propagated via a number of attack vectors, specifically targeted web servers and machines with Microsoft Windows operating systems.
- **SQL Slammer:** Using a flaw in Microsoft SQL Server, the quickly proliferating computer worm known as SQL Slammer caused network congestion and disruption.
- **Welchia**: In 2003, this worm unintentionally clogged networks while attempting to remove the Blaster worm from compromised systems and repair the exposed vulnerability.

Chapter 2: The Modern Cybersecurity Landscape

The current cybersecurity landscape is an ever-changing, difficult one that necessitates constant monitoring and response. To safeguard their digital assets and defend against cyber-attacks, firms must make investments in the newest technologies, put in place strong cybersecurity strategies, and promote a culture of security awareness.

The modern cybersecurity landscape is a dynamic and complicated one that brings both difficulties and opportunities in the ever-evolving world of technology. This chapter examines the salient features of the current cybersecurity landscape, such as new threats, developing technology, and methods used by businesses to safeguard their digital assets.

2.1. The Internet of Things (IoT) and Its Vulnerabilities

The Internet of Things (IoT) is a fast growing network of connected devices that gather, exchange, and process data often without any involvement from direct humans. While IoT has produced many breakthroughs and conveniences, it has also created a number of vulnerabilities that provide serious cybersecurity challenges. We'll look into the IoT devices' weaknesses in this part.

2.1.1. **Absence of Standards:** Lack of defined security standards is one of the main weaknesses in the IoT environment. Different businesses produce IoT devices, and many of them put utility and cost over strong security. As a result, there are many different security procedures used by various devices, which makes it challenging to set uniform security standards.

2.1.2. **Insufficient authentication and authorization:** Weak or default passwords are frequently used on IoT devices, and users hardly ever change them. Because of this, it is quite simple for hackers to access these devices via brute force methods or credential stuffing assaults. Furthermore, IoT devices frequently have weak authorisation systems that provide users or programs unneeded rights.

2.1.3. **Limited Memory and Processing Capacity**: IoT devices are often made with a restricted amount of memory and processing capacity to keep prices down and energy usage to a minimum. Implementing strong security mechanisms, including encryption and secure authentication, on these devices is difficult due to this restriction.

2.1.4. **Vulnerabilities in Firmware and Software**: IoT hardware frequently uses out-of-date or unpatched firmware and software. Manufacturers could fail to release timely patches or updates, leaving devices vulnerable to known flaws. These flaws can be used by attackers to take over IoT devices or obtain unauthorized access.

2.1.5. **Lack of Encryption**: Often, the encryption of data sent between IoT devices and servers is inadequate. Due to the lack of encryption, private information may be intercepted by nefarious parties, resulting in data breaches and privacy violations.

2.1.6. **Physical Vulnerabilities:** IoT devices are vulnerable to physical theft or tampering, giving Hackers access to the hardware directly. This may result in data extraction, reverse engineering, or the installation of malicious components.

2.1.7. **Supply Chain Risks**: Attackers have the potential to compromise IoT devices at different phases of the production process due to the complicated supply chain involved. This can entail altering the device's hardware or adding malware to the firmware.

2.1.8. **Lack of Security Updates**: Many IoT devices don't have a system in place for automatically downloading and installing security updates. Because of this, users might not be aware that updates are available or might find it difficult to update their devices even when they are.

2.1.9. **Network Vulnerabilities:** IoT devices frequently connect to private or public networks, and a breach on one device could result in an assault on the entire network. Vulnerabilities may be made worse by lax network security procedures, such as unprotected ports or unsecure Wi-Fi networks.

2.1.10. **Concerns about Privacy:** IoT devices gather a ton of information on people and their surroundings. When this data is managed improperly, shared without authorization, or made public due to security flaws, privacy problems arise.

Thus, the diversity of devices, lax security procedures, and resource limitations all contribute to the IoT ecosystem's weaknesses. Establishing and enforcing security standards, encouraging secure design principles, and educating users on the significance of IoT security are all necessary to address these vulnerabilities. This involves cooperation from device manufacturers, consumers, and regulatory agencies. Failure to do so could result in a more dangerous IoT environment, which could have serious repercussions for both people and businesses.

2.2. Mobile Devices and Security Challenges

These days, many firms place a high priority on mobile efforts since studies show that more mobility helps businesses increase operations and production. However, as corporate mobility rises, you may expect to see an increase in the number of mobile devices using remote connections to access your systems. As a result, your security teams will have a wider range of endpoints and threats to secure in order to safeguard your company from a data breach.

With the help of mobile devices like smartphones and tablets, people and businesses can stay connected, productive, and entertained in modern life. Due to their widespread use, portability, and sophistication, these devices do, however, also create a number of security challenges. The security issues posed by mobile devices will be discussed in this section.

2.2.1. **Diverse Ecosystems:** Mobile devices have different hardware setups and run a variety of operating systems, such as Android and iOS. Because vulnerabilities may affect different platforms differently due to this diversity, it is difficult for developers and security teams to offer universal protection

2.2.2. **App Stores and Malware**: While offering a regulated setting for the distribution of apps, app stores are not immune to malicious software. Malware can still make it onto app stores, and users may unintentionally download and install harmful programs that undermine the security and privacy of their device.

2.2.3. **Unpatched Devices**: It's possible that mobile device manufacturers and carriers occasionally fail to provide software updates and security fixes on schedule. Because of this, a lot of people use out-of-date operating systems and software, making their devices susceptible to known attacks.

2.2.4. **Jailbreaking and Rooting**: For more power and access to the operating system, some users decide to jailbreak (iOS) or root (Android) their devices. As a result, the device may be more vulnerable to viruses and potentially circumvent built-in security safeguards.

2.2.5. **Devices That Have Been Lost or Stolen**: Mobile devices are simple to lose or steal, and if suitable security measures, like strong passcodes or biometric authentication, are not in place, this could result in unauthorized access to critical information.

2.2.6. **Social Engineering Attacks**: Social engineering assaults like phishing and Smishing (SMS phishing) are particularly dangerous on mobile devices. These strategies can be used by attackers to persuade users into disclosing private information or downloading dangerous software.

2.2.7. **Unsecured Wi-Fi Networks**: Insecure or hacked Wi-Fi networks are frequently connected to by mobile devices. Devices are more vulnerable to data interception and man-in-the-middle attacks when connected to insecure networks.

2.2.8. **Data Breach and Privacy Issues:** Mobile apps routinely ask for permission to access a variety of user data, including as location, contacts, and camera data. Ineffective data exchange and management of app permissions can lead to privacy violations and data leaks.

2.2.9. **BYOD (Bring Your Own Device) Policies**: The implementation of BYOD rules in corporate settings may pose security risks. Employees might use personal devices for work-related tasks, thereby increasing the danger to sensitive corporate data.

2.2.10. **Risks of Mobile Banking and Payment**: Mobile devices are being used as wallets and banking tools more and more, which makes them appealing targets for financial fraud. To safeguard user accounts and transactions, mobile payment apps and banking applications need to employ strong security features.

Therefore, because of their distinctive features and the constantly changing threat landscape, mobile devices are vulnerable to a wide range of security issues. To reduce these dangers, users and companies must be proactive. These actions include keeping devices up to date, maintaining good app hygiene, using strong authentication techniques, and being watchful for social engineering attacks. Mobile devices will continue to be essential for both personal and professional activity, hence mobile security will be a crucial issue.

2.3. Cloud Computing and Cybersecurity

The term "cloud" or, more precisely, "cloud computing" refers to the method of gaining access to materials, programs, and databases via the Internet and outside the constraints of local hardware. Utilizing this technology allows businesses to scale their operations with greater flexibility by transferring the majority or a portion of the management of their infrastructure to external hosting companies.

The cloud computing services that are most popular and extensively used are:

- **IaaS (Infrastructure-as-a-Service)**: This is a hybrid method in which businesses can manage some of their data and applications on-premises while entrusting cloud service providers to take care of their server, hardware, networking, virtualization, and storage requirements.
- **PaaS (Platform-as-a-Service):** Provides a unique application architecture that automatically controls operating systems, software upgrades, storage, and supporting infrastructure. This allows enterprises to streamline the development and delivery of their applications.
- **SaaS (Software-as-a-Service):** Refers to cloud-based applications that are hosted online and often made available via subscription. The management of all potential technical concerns by third parties, including data, middleware, servers, and storage, reduces the use of IT resources and streamlines upkeep and support tasks.

2.3.1. What Makes Cloud Security Crucial? The adoption of cloud-based environments and IaaS, PaaS, or SaaS computing models has increased in contemporary organizations. When organizations effectively resource their departments, the dynamic nature of infrastructure management, particularly in scaling applications and services, can present a number of issues. Organizations can outsource many of the time-consuming IT-related duties thanks to these as-a-service models. Understanding the security standards for keeping data safe has become essential as businesses continue to shift to the cloud.

Although third-party cloud computing service providers might take over the management of this infrastructure, the accountability and security of data assets may not necessarily move with it. The majority of cloud service providers actively maintain the integrity of their servers by default adhering to standard security practices. When it comes to safeguarding data, applications, and workloads that are hosted in the cloud, enterprises must take their unique factors into account.

With the continued development of the digital environment, security concerns have advanced. Due to an organization's general lack of visibility in data access and movement, these risks specifically target suppliers of cloud computing. Organizations may encounter serious governance and compliance issues when handling client information, regardless of where it is housed, if they don't take proactive measures to increase their cloud security.

No matter the size of your company, cloud security needs to be a major talking point. Almost every aspect of contemporary computing is supported by cloud infrastructure, which spans several verticals and all sectors. However, putting in place sufficient defenses against contemporary cyberattacks is essential for a successful cloud adoption. Cloud security is essential regardless of whether your company uses a public, private, or hybrid cloud.

The way businesses manage and provide IT services has been completely transformed by cloud computing. Scalability, flexibility, and cost-effectiveness are provided, but it also creates new cybersecurity challenges. We'll look at the connection between cloud computing and cybersecurity in this part.

2.3.2. **Data Security**: Strong data security measures are needed when storing sensitive data in the cloud. In order to prevent illegal access, companies must manage encryption keys and access controls properly. Cloud providers often offer encryption at rest and in transit.

2.3.3. **Identity and Access Management (IAM)**: In a cloud environment, controlling user access and permissions can be challenging. In order to avoid unwanted access and data breaches, it is essential to implement sound IAM policies, such as strong authentication procedures and least privilege access.

2.3.4. **Shared Responsibility Model:** The majority of cloud service providers operate under a shared responsibility model, which means that while they are in charge of protecting the underlying infrastructure, customers are in charge of protecting their own data and applications. Effective cloud cybersecurity requires an understanding of this division of labour.

2.3.5. **Compliance with Laws and Regulations**: When employing cloud services, organizations must manage a variety of compliance obligations, including GDPR, HIPAA, and industry-specific rules. For cloud services to operate legally and profitably, compliance with these laws must be ensured.

2.3.6. **Data Breach**: Misconfigurations, internal risks, and outside attacks can all lead to data breaches in the cloud. To lessen the effects of breaches and minimize data disclosure, quick identification and action are crucial.

2.2.7. **DDoS (Distributed Denial of Service) Attacks**: DDoS attacks can affect cloud-based software and services. DDoS mitigation services are frequently provided by cloud providers, but enterprises must configure and maintain them to be protected.

2.2.8. **Vendor Lock-In**: Businesses that depend heavily on one cloud provider may experience vendor lock-in, which makes switching to another provider or going back to an on-premises environment challenging. This risk can be reduced by making preparations for multi-cloud or hybrid cloud systems.

2.2.9. **Data Transfer Security**: Data that is being transferred to and from the cloud may be intercepted. Encryption and secure data transfer protocols, such as SSL/TLS, are necessary to safeguard data while it is in transit.

2.2.10. **Shadow IT**: Without IT's awareness, staff members could use unlawful cloud services and applications, resulting in security gaps. Shadow IT monitoring and cloud security policy implementation can assist in reducing this risk.

2.3.11 **Incidence Response**: It is essential to create and evaluate an incident response plan tailored for cloud systems. How to handle security occurrences and data breaches in the cloud should be covered in this plan.

2.3.12. **Security as Code**: Integrating security into the development and deployment pipelines is a crucial part of adopting DevSecOps processes in the cloud. This makes sure that security is considered from the beginning of the application development process.

Thus, cloud computing has many advantages but also brings particular cybersecurity difficulties. Organizations must take a proactive and comprehensive approach to cloud security, which includes realizing that they share responsibility with cloud providers, putting in place effective access controls, adhering to applicable laws, and regularly assessing and enhancing their cloud security posture. To safeguard data, apps, and infrastructure in the digital age, effective cloud security is crucial.

2.4. Social Engineering and Human Factors

Attacks using social engineering trick individuals into paying money to criminals, sending information they shouldn't transmit, installing software they shouldn't download, visiting websites they shouldn't visit, and other security-related blunders. Social engineering is frequently referred to as "human hacking" since it involves psychological manipulation and preys on human fallibility or weakness rather than technical or digital system flaws. Just a few examples of social engineering include an email that appears to be from a trusted coworker and requests private information, a menacing voicemail purporting to be from the IRS, and an offer of riches from a foreign potentate.

Cybercriminals frequently employ social engineering techniques to acquire personal or financial data, such as login credentials, credit card numbers, bank account numbers, and Social Security numbers. With this information, they can commit identity theft and make purchases with other people's money or credit, apply for loans in other people's names, apply for other people's unemployment benefits, and more. However, a social engineering attack could also be the precursor to a more significant strike. For instance, a hacker might coerce a victim into giving a login and password, then use those details to infect the victim's employer's network with ransomware.

Cybercriminals are drawn to social engineering because it allows them to access digital networks, devices, and accounts without having to perform the challenging technical effort required to bypass firewalls.

Thus, Social engineering is the term used to describe the manipulation of people to get sensitive information, carry out tasks, or undermine security systems. Instead than taking advantage of technical flaws, it manipulates human psychology. Protecting against cyber-attacks requires an understanding of social engineering and its different methods:

The idea of social engineering is examined in this section along with how it affects cybersecurity.

2.4.1. **Phishing**: One of the most popular types of social engineering is phishing. Attackers deceive receivers into divulging important information, such as passwords or financial information, by sending false emails, messages, or websites that seem authentic.

2.4.2. **Spear Phishing**: Spear phishing is a specific type of phishing in which attackers conduct victim research to create messages that are tailored specifically for them. These emails frequently come out as quite trustworthy and have a higher chance of tricking their intended recipients.

2.4.3. **Pretexting**: Pretexting is the act of fabricating a situation or pretext to persuade someone to divulge information or take an action. This frequently entails pretending to be a respected person or an authority figure.

2.4.4. **Temptation**: Baiting is the practice of luring people with an alluring offer or free download in order to persuade them to click on harmful links or download malware.

2.4.5. **Tailgating (Piggybacking)**: When an attacker follows a legitimate individual closely, they are said to be tailgating in a physical sense. This allows them to obtain access to a secure place without authorization. This approach takes advantage of lack of verification and common courtesy.

2.4.6. **Quid Pro Quo**: Attackers ask for information in exchange for a promise of something. For instance, they can pretend to be IT help and ask for login information in exchange for fixing a problem that doesn't exist.

2.4.7. **Impersonation:** Impersonation is the act of feigning another person's identity, whether in person, over the phone, or online.

Attackers may pretend to be co-workers, executives, or service providers in order to obtain confidence and access to private data.

2.4.8. **Psychological Manipulation**: Social engineers persuade people into complying with their demands through psychological strategies including fear, urgency, authority, or empathy.

2.4.9. **Human Error**: Cybersecurity is significantly influenced by human factors. Breach points can be caused by errors including poor passwords, unintentional data disclosure, and improperly configured security settings.

2.4.10. **Education and Information**: A vital line of defence is educating people about the dangers and strategies of social engineering. Employees who have received security awareness training are better able to identify and resist social engineering tricks.

2.4.11. **Multi-Factor Authentication (MFA):** By demanding several forms of verification, MFA adds an extra layer of security and decreases the likelihood of unwanted access even if credentials are stolen.

2.4.12. **Security Policies and Procedures**: To effectively combat social engineering threats, organizations should set up and implement defined security policies, practices, and incident response plans.

2.4.13. **Verification and Scepticism**: Many social engineering schemes can be avoided by advising people to confirm the legitimacy of people or institutions asking sensitive information and to use a healthy dose of scepticism.

In conclusion, social engineering attacks take use of the human factor in cybersecurity and can be quite successful. Technology, education, policies, and a security-conscious culture must all be used to combat social engineering. Organizations can greatly lessen their susceptibility to social engineering attacks and improve overall cybersecurity by addressing these aspects.

Chapter 3: Emerging Trends in Cyberattacks

The environment of cyber threats is always shifting, posing new difficulties for both individuals and companies. In an increasingly linked world, it is crucial to manage these developing risks and secure digital assets by staying educated about new patterns in cyberattacks and implementing proactive cybersecurity measure.

Cybercriminals are continuously coming up with new strategies and methods to exploit weaknesses, which is why the cybersecurity landscape is constantly changing. This chapter examines a few of the new patterns in cyberattacks and offers insights into how these threats are always evolving.

2.1. Advanced Persistent Threats (APTs)

Advanced Persistent Threats (APTs) are a group of highly skilled and focused cyberattacks that are distinguished by their stealth, persistence, and the substantial resources and experience needed to carry them out. APTs are often planned by threat actors with sufficient resources and motivation, such as nation-states, criminal gangs, or hacktivist collectives.

We'll go into the essential traits and components of APTs in this section.

2.1.1. **Long-Term Focus:** APTs are painstakingly planned and carried out with a long-term perspective; they are not opportunistic attacks. Threat actors are prepared to devote time and resources to breaking into a target system or organization.

2.1.2. **Discretion and Stealth**: APTs frequently compromise a target's defences without setting off alarms or alerts in an effort to go undetected for long periods of time. Attackers can keep access and gradually amass useful information thanks to this stealth.

2.1.3. **Customisation**: APTs are targeted attacks where the attackers do in-depth reconnaissance to learn about the infrastructure, personnel, and weaknesses of the target. The possibility of success is increased by this adjustment.

2.1.4. **Multiple Attack Vectors**: Spear-phishing emails, malware, zero-day exploits, supply chain intrusions, and social engineering techniques are just a few of the assault methods used by APTs. The odds of infiltration are increased by these various strategies.

2.1.5. **Data Exfiltration**: Exfiltrating sensitive information or intellectual property over an extended period of time is one of APTs' main goals. Attackers frequently remain active in order to continue gathering important data.

2.1.6. **Infrastructure for Command and Control (C2):** APTs create C2 infrastructure that enables them to remotely manipulate infected systems. The fact that this infrastructure is frequently fragmented makes it challenging for defenders to locate and destroy.

2.1.7. **Evasion and Countermeasures**: APTs employ evasion strategies to get around security tools including firewalls, intrusion detection systems, and antivirus software. They actively try to avoid being discovered while adapting to defence mechanisms.

2.1.8. **Nation-State Actors**: Nation-state actors seeking geopolitical, commercial, or intelligence goals are said to be responsible for some APTs. The resources and capabilities of these state-sponsored APTs are frequently vast.

2.1.9. **Persistent Access:** Keeping persistent access to infiltrated systems is a crucial component of APTs. APTs are built to regain control through secondary or backup means even if the initial access is lost.

2.1.10. **Secret Activities**: Because APTs work covertly, it can be difficult for victims to realize they have been hacked. As a result, these attacks frequently go undiagnosed for long periods of time.

2.1.11. **Espionage and Counterintelligence**: APTs are frequently linked to espionage and the theft of sensitive material, including classified information, government secrets, and intellectual property.

2.1.12. **Attribution Challenges**: Due to the usage of proxies, hacked systems, and false flags, pinpointing the source of APTs can be quite challenging. An intricate task that might involve intelligence agencies and cybersecurity professionals is accurate attribution.

In conclusion, advanced persistent threats are a persistent and highly specialized type of cyberattack that provide serious difficulties for governments and enterprises. Strong cybersecurity defences, threat intelligence, and the capacity to change course when necessary are all necessary for combating sophisticated threat actors like APTs.

2.2. Zero-Day Exploits

A substantial and developing danger to cybersecurity is posed by zero-day exploits. These exploits go after flaws in hardware or software that neither the vendor nor the general public are aware of. The main characteristics of zero-day exploits and their significance for cybersecurity will be discussed in this section.

2.2.1. **What are Zero-Day Exploits?**: An attack known as a "zero-day exploit" makes use of a flaw in a software program, operating system, or hardware component the same day it is made public, giving the manufacturer no time to fix the problem.

2.2.2. **Zero-Day Exploits - Characteristics**:

- *Unpatched Vulnerabilities:* Zero-day vulnerabilities are those for which there is no official patch or remedy available.
- *Covert and Stealthy*: Because security providers and organizations are not aware of the vulnerability, these attacks are frequently covert and challenging to detect.
- *High Value:* Zero-day exploits can be exploited for targeted attacks, espionage, or financial gain and are extremely desirable on the black market.

1. **Zero-Day Lifecycle**:

- *Discovery:* The vulnerability is found by a security researcher, an evildoer, or a group, but they keep it quiet.
- *Exploitation:* Attackers use the vulnerability to breach a system or obtain unauthorized access by exploiting it.
- *Disclosure:* The vendor or the general public eventually learns about the vulnerability. This might occur as a result of the

discoverer making a responsible disclosure, a breach, or independent investigation.

- *Patch Development*: When a vendor is made aware of a vulnerability, they create a patch or update to address it.
- *Patch Distribution*: Users are urged to install the patch in order to safeguard their systems.

1. **Impact And Risk**:

- Zero-day exploits have the potential to cause serious problems, such as data breaches, system compromises, and the proliferation of malware.
- High-profile assaults utilizing zero-day vulnerabilities can cause harm to an organization's reputation, financial losses, and legal implications.

1. **Nation-State and APT**: Zero-day exploits are frequently used by nation-state actors and Advanced Persistent Threat (APT) groups for specialized assaults, espionage, and cyberwarfare. Geopolitical and ethical issues are raised by the possibility that governments may store zero-days for offensive uses.
2. **Defensive Measures**:

- *Vulnerability Management*: Organizations should put strong vulnerability management processes in place to find and fix vulnerabilities before they are used against them.
- *Patch Management:* helps reduce the risk of zero-day exploits via timely application of security fixes and updates.
- *Intrusion Detection:* Network monitoring and intrusion detection systems can be used to spot odd behaviour and zero-day assaults.
- *Threat Intelligence*: For proactive defence, it's essential to keep up with new threats and zero-day vulnerabilities using threat intelligence sources.

1. **Ethical Considerations**: Zero-day vulnerabilities have recently been discovered, which raises ethical concerns about responsible disclosure, responsible use by governments, and the overall goal of cybersecurity.

In summary, zero-day exploits pose a significant threat to cybersecurity because of their high impact potential, stealth, and use by both cybercriminals and state-sponsored actors. To reduce the dangers posed by zero-day vulnerabilities, organizations must prioritize proactive security measures, vulnerability management, and threat intelligence. How these vulnerabilities are handled and shared within the cybersecurity community also depends on ethical concerns.

2.3. Fileless Malware

Malicious software that functions in memory and leaves no typical traces on a victim's file system is known as "*Fileless Malware*," and it is a sneaky and pervasive type of malware. For cybersecurity experts, this kind of malware poses special difficulties. We shall examine the traits, methods, and ramifications of fileless malware in this section.

2.3.1. Characteristics of Fileless Malware:

- *No File Presence*: Malware that lacks files does not use the usual executable files or scripts that are stored on the victim's drive. It only uses memory, which makes it harder to identify using file-based scanning.
- *Memory-Based Execution:* This sort of malware works by immediately executing in the volatile memory (RAM) of a computer, from where it can perform harmful operations without storing data on the hard drive.
- *Stealth and Evasion:* Because fileless malware frequently makes use of legitimate system functions and tools, it is more difficult to detect using conventional antivirus software or endpoint security solutions.
- *Living-off-the-Land:* Attackers use reputable programs and system utilities to run their malicious code while blending in with regular system activities.

1. **Methods Fileless Malware Employs**:

- *PowerShell and Scripting Language*: Attackers frequently employ scripting languages, such as PowerShell or JavaScript, to execute malicious code immediately in memory.
- *Living-Off-The-Land Binaries*: Using trusted system executables and tools, such Windows Management

Instrumentation (WMI) or Windows Management Instrumentation Command-line (WMIC), malicious actors can launch assaults. This technique is known as "living-off-the-land binaries."

- *Reflective Injection*: To avoid detection, fileless malware can inject harmful code straight into an active process, frequently one that is already reliable and trusted.
- *Registry-Based Attacks*: Some fileless malware stores and runs dangerous code in the Windows Registry, making it difficult to find and delete.
- *Malicious Macros*: By taking advantage of the fact that Microsoft Word and Excel files are trusted, malicious macros can be used to distribute fileless malware.

1. **Implications and Challenges:**

- **Stealth and Evasion**: Because fileless malware doesn't leave behind conventional file artefacts, it is famously difficult to identify and delete.
- **Detection and Prevention:** Fileless malware is more resistant to traditional signature-based antivirus programs. Heuristic detection methods and behavioural analysis become essential.
- **Persistence:** Fileless malware has the ability to build persistence mechanisms on the infected machine, enabling it to withstand reboots and security measures.
- Privilege Escalation: Once in memory, fileless malware may attempt to increase privileges and migrate laterally across a network, which might potentially result in extensive damage.

1. **Defence and Mitigation Techniques**:

- **Endpoint Detection and Response (EDR)**: EDR systems can keep an eye out for indications of malicious activity by monitoring system and process behaviour, giving visibility into fileless attacks.

- **User Education and Awareness:** Informing users of the dangers of opening email attachments or turning on macros can aid in halting the spread of the infection.
- **Least Privilege Access**: By limiting user and system privileges, fileless malware's capacity to operate can be constrained.
- **Patch Management:** reduces vulnerabilities that fileless malware may exploit by keeping systems and software up to date.
- **Network Segmentation**: By isolating crucial systems and dividing network traffic into different segments, fileless malware can't spread laterally as much.

In summary, because fileless malware is stealthy and can bypass conventional security procedures, it poses a serious and developing threat to cybersecurity. Organizations need to utilize sophisticated detection methods, maintain high endpoint security, and train users to identify and reduce the threats posed by fileless malware.

2.4. Supply Chain Attacks

Cyberattacks of the type known as supply chain attacks aim to compromise an organization's partners, suppliers, or service providers. These assaults have become more well-known in recent years because of their potential for wide-ranging effects and their difficulty in being identified and mitigated.

We will examine the main traits, methods, and effects of supply chain attacks in this section.

2.4.1. **Characteristics Of Supply Chain Attacks:**

- *Third-Party Compromise*: In supply chain assaults, reputable third parties who do business with the target enterprise are compromised.
- *Trusted Access*: Attackers use the relationship of trust that has been built up between them and the target organization to access its computer systems or data.
- *Impact from an Indirect Source*: The main objective of supply chain attacks is to compromise the target organization through the infrastructure or software of the supply chain partner.

1. **Techniques Employed in Supply Chain Attacks:**

- *Malicious Software Insertion*: To introduce malware or backdoors, attackers may corrupt software updates or supply chain components. The malware enters the environment of the target organization when these updates are implemented.
- *Credential Theft*: Using valid login credentials to avoid detection, cybercriminals may steal credentials from a supply chain partner in order to access the target organization's systems.

- *Counterfeit Hardware or Software*: Hardware or software that is counterfeit or tampered with can be introduced into the supply chain by attackers, creating vulnerabilities or backdoors when these components are used.
- *Man-in-the-Middle Attacks*: By listening in on conversations between the target company and its partners in the supply chain, attackers can insert malicious code or change data.
- *Watering Hole Attacks:* Attackers hack a website or other resource that the staff or partners of the target organization routinely access. People who visit the infected website might unintentionally download dangerous payloads.

1. **Implications and Difficulties:**

- *Impact:* Attacks on the supply chain can have a wide-ranging impact, possibly affecting not only the target firm but also those organizations farther down the supply chain.
- *Challenges in Detection*: Since the initial penetration frequently takes place outside the target organization's network, detecting supply chain hacks can be challenging.
- *Attribution Challenges*: Identifying the origin of a supply chain assault can be difficult because of the participation of numerous parties and the possibility of obfuscation.
- *Reputation Damage:* Supply chain assaults can undermine the target organization's credibility and reputation, which can result in financial losses and client attrition.

1. **Strategies for Defence and Mitigation:**

- **Vendor Risk Assessment**: Evaluate the cybersecurity practices of supply chain partners, taking into account their security procedures, capability for handling security incidents, and incident response skills.
- **Secure Communication:** To protect sensitive information shared with supply chain partners, use secure communication

channels, such as encrypted data exchanges.

- **Third-Party Security Audits**: To find weaknesses and potential hazards, conduct security audits and assessments of third-party vendors and service providers.
- **Software Validation**: Verify the validity and integrity of software updates and components before integrating them into the systems used by your company.
- **Network Segmentation**: In the event of a supply chain compromise, isolate and separate crucial systems to restrict attacker lateral movement.
- **Incident Response Planning**: Develop an incident response strategy that addresses how to respond to supply chain assaults, including contacting and working with impacted partners.

In summary, supply chain attacks are a serious and developing threat that prey on businesses by taking advantage of the trust they have built up with their partners and suppliers. For vital assets and data to be protected and the potential effects of supply chain assaults to be minimized, proactive risk assessment, security measures, and incident response preparation are required.

2.5. State-Sponsored Cyberattacks

Cyber operations carried out or sponsored by governments or state bodies are referred to as state-sponsored cyberattacks, nation-state cyberattacks, or advanced persistent threats (APTs). These assaults frequently target political, economic, or military targets and are well-funded and highly sophisticated. We shall examine the main traits, causes, methods, and effects of state-sponsored cyberattacks in this section.

3.5.1. **State-Sponsored Cyberattacks' Characteristics**

- **Government Support**: Government or state entities offer significant resources, such as cash, skill, and infrastructure, to support or carry out these attacks.
- **Long-term Perspective**: State-sponsored cyberattacks frequently have a long-term outlook and concentrate on persistent access, intelligence gathering, and strategic objectives.
- **Stealth and Sophistication**: These assaults frequently use cutting-edge methods to avoid detection and attribution. They are typically very clever.
- **Diverse Objectives**: State-sponsored cyberattacks may have a variety of goals in mind, such as influence campaigns, data theft, disruption of vital infrastructure, and espionage.
- **Political or Geopolitical Motivations:** State-sponsored cyberattacks are frequently motivated by political or geopolitical factors, such as the advancement of national interests, intelligence gathering, or geopolitical benefit.

    1. **The Reasons Behind State-Sponsored Cyberattacks**:

- **Espionage**: Gathering information on political, military, economic, or scientific advancements in other countries is a typical goal of espionage.

- **Economic Gain**: Businesses or sectors may be the target of state-sponsored cyberattacks intended to steal intellectual property, trade secrets, or a competitive edge.
- **Political Influence**: State-sponsored initiatives often include attempts to sway public opinion, sabotage elections, or cause strife between competing states.
- **Military And Strategic Goals**: During times of conflict, key infrastructure, such as power grids or communication networks, may be disrupted or rendered inoperable by cyberattacks.

1. **Cyberattack Methods Employed by State Sponsored Attacks:**

- **Zero-Day Exploits:** Nation-state actors frequently own or buy zero-day exploits to target particular software vulnerabilities.
- **Advanced Malware**: Complex malware is used to compromise and remain on target computers, such as specially created APTs.
- **Supply Chain Attacks**: State-sponsored actors may enter vital systems through the supply chain and install backdoors, modified hardware, or malicious software.
- **Spear phishing:** Campaigns that are specifically targeted at a target send harmful payloads to selected people or groups within the target.
- **Watering Hole Attacks**: Criminals access websites that their target audience frequently visits in order to infect users with malware.

1. **Implications and Difficulties:**

- **Geopolitical Tensions**: State-sponsored cyberattacks have the potential to exacerbate international tensions and have negative diplomatic or economic repercussions.

- **Challenges in Attribution**: Because of the use of proxies, false flags, and obfuscation techniques, it can be difficult to identify which states are the targets of state-sponsored cyberattacks.
- **Impact on Critical Infrastructure**: Attacks on critical infrastructure can have serious real-world repercussions that compromise national security and threaten public safety.
- **International Law and Norms**: Cyberattacks by states frequently raise concerns about adherence to international law and standards regulating cyberspace conflict.

1. **Strategies for Defence and Mitigation:**

- *Advanced Cybersecurity Measures*: Organizations and governments must use advanced cybersecurity measures, such as capabilities for intrusion detection, threat intelligence, and incident response.
- *International Cooperation*: State-sponsored cyber threats must be addressed, and international norms must be established, through diplomatic initiatives and cooperation.
- *Resilience and Redundancy:* Critical infrastructure should be built with redundancy and resilience in order to withstand cyberattacks and sustain essential services.
- *Attribution and Deterrence*: Governments and organizations should work to enhance attribution capabilities and take deterrence measures into consideration in order to deter state-sponsored attacks.

In summary, state-sponsored cyberattacks represent a substantial and intricate class of cyber threats with important geopolitical ramifications. A combination of cutting-edge cybersecurity solutions, international collaboration, and initiatives to develop standards of responsible behaviour in cyberspace are needed to defend against these attacks.

3.5.6. The Most Prevalent Types And Classes Of Cyberattacks

Type of Cyber Attack	Attack Description	Common Targets	Examples of Mitigation Strategies
1. **Phishing**	Deceptive emails or messages to trick recipients into revealing sensitive information or clicking on malicious links.	Individuals and Organizations.	Employee training on recognizing phishing attempts. Use email filtering and authentication protocols. Multi-factor authentication (MFA) for account access.
1. **Ransomware**	Encrypts user data and demands a ransom for decryption.	Individuals and Organizations.	Regular data backups stored offline. Patch and update software and systems regularly. Use endpoint protection solutions.
1. **Distributed Denial of Service (DDoS)**	Overwhelms a target system or network with excessive traffic, causing it to become unavailable.	Websites and Online Services.	Implement DDoS mitigation solutions and services.

			Use content delivery networks (CDNs) for traffic distribution Monitor network traffic for unusual patterns.
1. **Malware**	Malicious software that can infect and compromise computers and networks.	Individuals and Organizations.	Install reputable antivirus and anti-malware software. Keep software and operating systems updated. Educate users on safe downloading and software installation.
1. **Insider Threats**	Attacks initiated or facilitated by individuals or entities within the organization.	Organizations	Implement access controls and user monitoring Conduct background checks and security training

			for employees. Use data loss prevention (DLP) solutions
1. **Man-In-the-Middle (MitM) Attacks**	Intercepts and potentially alters communications between two parties without their knowledge	Any communications	Use encryption for data in transit (e.g., HTTPS). Verify digital certificates and use secure channels for communication. Educate users on recognizing suspicious activities.
1. **SQL Injection**	Exploits vulnerabilities in SQL databases to inject malicious SQL queries, potentially gaining access to sensitive data.	Web Applications	Input validation and parameterized queries in code Regularly update and patch web application software. Implement web application firewalls (WAFs).
	Attacks that target	Various	Promptly apply

1. **Zero-Day-Exploits**	vulnerabilities in software or hardware that are not yet known to the vendor or the public.	security patches and updates. Employ intrusion detection and prevention systems (IDS/IPS). Engage with vendors and threat intelligence sources for alerts.

Figure 2: Some of the most prevalent types and classes of cyberattacks

Note: Cyberattacks are diverse and can encompass many variations and techniques. Mitigation strategies should be tailored to the specific threats an organization faces and should include a combination of technical measures, user training, and proactive security measures.

Chapter 4: The Cost of Cyberattacks

Depending on the type and scope of the attack, the target, and the efficacy of the cybersecurity measures in place, the cost of cyberattacks can vary significantly. A multifaceted strategy that incorporates cybersecurity best practices, incident response planning, employee training, and ongoing risk assessment is needed to prevent intrusions and lessen their impact. Organizations and governments need to fully understand the costs of cyberattacks in order to make educated choices about cybersecurity investments and risk management tactics.

Cyberattacks can be expensive, resulting in both direct and indirect costs. These expenses may have an impact on people, corporations, governments, and society at large. For assessing the impact of these threats and putting appropriate cybersecurity measures in place, it is crucial to comprehend the different costs associated with cyberattacks.

The following are some important elements that affect how much money cyberattacks cost:

4.1. Financial Losses

An important portion of the entire cost of cyberattacks is financial losses. Cybercriminals employ a number of strategies to financially hurt people, companies, and organizations directly or indirectly.

Each year, computer viruses cost the economy billions of dollars in losses. As a result, a market for antivirus software has emerged, offering or giving away virus protection to users of different operating systems.

We will look at the many kinds of financial damages brought on by cyberattacks in this section:

4.1.1. Stolen Funds:

- *Bank Account Hacks*: Hacks into bank accounts give cybercriminals the opportunity to steal money or carry out fraudulent transactions by gaining unauthorized access to people's or companies' bank accounts.
- *Cryptocurrency Theft*: Digital assets like Bitcoin or Ethereum can be stolen when cryptocurrency exchanges and wallets are targeted.
- *Payment fraud*: Unauthorized purchases can be made using credit card information obtained through data breaches or phishing scams.

4.1.2. Ransom Payments:

- **Ransomware Attacks**: In order to restore access to their data or systems, victims of ransomware attacks may decide to pay the perpetrators a ransom. These payments can be significant and there is no assurance that the data will be recovered.

4.1.3. Business Disruption:

- **Costs of Downtime:** System hacks or distributed denial of service (DDoS) attacks can cause business disruptions and a loss of revenue.
- **Operational Impact:** Disrupted operations, including e-commerce platforms, online services, and industrial processes, can lead to lost income.

4.1.4. Fraud and Identity Theft

- **Financial Fraud**: Cyberattacks frequently result in financial fraud, such as check fraud, wire fraud, and illegal credit card transactions.
- **Identity Theft:** When personal information is stolen, it can be used to commit identity theft, costing victims money as they work to restore their credit and identities.

4.1.5. Legal and Regulatory Fees:

- **Legal Fees:** May be incurred by organizations as a result of cyber incidents. These costs may include engaging legal counsel, carrying out investigations, and pursuing legal action.
- **Regulatory Penalties**: Violations of data protection laws like the GDPR or HIPAA can result in significant fines and penalties.

4.1.6. Data Recovery:

- **Costs of Data Restoration**: Recovering and restoring corrupted data can be expensive, especially if backups are either unavailable or corrupted as well.
- **Data Loss:** In some circumstances, data may be lost forever, causing the loss of important knowledge and intellectual property.

4.1.7. Costs of Insurance:

- **Cyber Insurance Premiums**: Even when an organization has cyber insurance, it may still have to pay premiums and deductibles after a cyber catastrophe.

4.1.8. Supply Chain Disruption:

- **Production Delays:** Attacks on service providers or suppliers can stymie an organization's supply chain, causing production delays and extra expenditures.
- **Cost Increases:** Businesses might have to pay more to get goods or services from alternative providers.

In summary, there can be a wide range of direct and indirect costs associated with cyberattacks that affect both people and businesses. These losses could include money taken, ransom payments, interruption of company, expenditures associated with legal and regulatory proceedings, data recovery fees, and more. It takes a mix of strong cybersecurity safeguards, incident response planning, personnel training, and insurance coverage to mitigate these financial risks.

4.2. Reputational Damage

An important component of the cost of cyberattacks, especially for corporations and organizations, is reputational damage. Customer trust, brand image, and market value can all be adversely affected by the effect of a cyber event on an entity's reputation. We shall discuss the idea of reputational harm brought on by cyberattacks in this section.

4.2.1. Impact on Brand and Reputation:

- **Loss of Trust**: Cyberattacks reduce stakeholder and customer confidence in a company's capacity to safeguard sensitive data, including personal information, financial information, and intellectual property.
- **Customer Perception**: Bad press resulting from a data breach or security issue can affect a customer's loyalty and retention by creating a poor perception of the company.
- **Brand Image Damage**: A company's reputation and brand image can be damaged, which reduces brand value and market competitiveness.

1. **Customer Churn**

- **Loss of Customers**: In the wake of a high-profile cyber incident, some clients may decide to cut connections with the impacted company and turn to rivals they believe to be much safer.
- **Costs of Customer Acquisition**: Getting new consumers to replace lost ones may be costly and time-consuming, and it often requires marketing initiatives and incentives to do so.

1. **The Stock Market's Effect on Money:**

- **Stock Price Decrease**: As investors react to news of a cyber event, the stock prices of publicly traded corporations may decrease.

- **Loss in Market Capitalization**: Lower stock prices might lead to a drop in market capitalization, which could result in financial losses for the company.

1. **Regulatory Examination**

- **Investigations by Regulatory Agencies**: For failing to comply with data protection regulations, regulatory bodies may conduct investigations into cyber events.
- **Public Disclosure**: Organizations might be obliged to make data breaches public, which would harm their reputation even more.

1. **Class-Action Lawsuits:**

- **Legal action**: Victims of the breach or other interested parties may file class-action lawsuits against the organization.
- **Legal Fees**: Fighting lawsuits and settlements can cost a lot of money in legal fees.

1. **Operational Impact:**

- **Disrupted Operations:** Operational disruptions brought on by cyberattacks can result in client discontent, contract cancellations, and financial loss for a business.

Effects on the Supply Chain: Relationships between the impacted firm and its vendors and supply chain partners may suffer as a result of reputational harm.

4.2.7. Long-Term Repercussions

- **Reputation Damage**: Reputational harm can have long-term effects, damaging a company's position in the market and its brand for years after the initial incident.

- **Rebuilding Trust**: It takes time and resources to rebuild trust and heal a damaged reputation.

To sum up, one of the most costly and long-lasting effects of cyberattacks on firms can be reputational harm. The cost of cyber events as a whole includes lost customer trust, brand harm, financial effect, legal repercussions, and operational disruption. Effective cybersecurity safeguards, incident response, proactive communication, transparency, and attempts to re-establish stakeholder trust are all necessary for reputational harm mitigation.

4.3. Legal and Regulatory Consequences

Legal and regulatory consequences are the possible legal actions, fines, or outcomes that people, groups, or institutions may experience as a result of breaking laws, rules, or legal requirements. Depending on the particular violation, the jurisdiction in which it occurs, and the seriousness of the offense, these consequences can differ greatly.

Here are a few such legal and regulatory repercussions:

4.3.1. **Fines and Penalties:** There may be financial repercussions for breaking laws and regulations. These fines may be quite little for transgressions that are not very significant or they may be very large for violations that are very serious. The nature and severity of the offense, as well as the relevant legislation, are among the elements that frequently affect the fine's precise amount.

4.3.2. **Civil Lawsuits**: May be brought against people or organizations who negligently cause harm to another person. If these actions are successful, the harmed person may receive compensation.

4.3.3. **Criminal Charges:** A few infractions of the law and regulations are prosecutable as crimes. If found guilty, defendants could be sentenced to jail time, probation, or other harsh punishments. Additionally, businesses may be charged with crimes and liable to fines or other penalties.

4.3.4. **Regulatory Sanctions**: Regulatory authorities have the power to impose a range of sanctions, including revocation of licenses, permits, or certificates; suspension of operations; or increased regulatory scrutiny of an entity.

4.3.5. **Legal Action by Regulatory Authorities**: Regulatory agencies with the power to prosecute those who break their rules include the Environmental Protection Agency (EPA), Securities and Exchange Commission (SEC), and Food and Drug Administration (FDA). Injunctions, fines, and other legal sanctions are examples of this.

4.3.6. **Compliance Orders:** Regulatory authorities have the authority to issue compliance orders, which call for particular actions to be taken by people or organizations in order to correct infractions. Further legal action may be taken if these directions are not followed.

4.3.7. **Reputational Damage:** Legal and regulatory repercussions can cause serious reputational damage, which can lower a person's or an organization's standing in the community or industry.

4.3.8. **Revocation of a License or Permit:** Is a common practice for many professions and enterprises. Revocation of these licenses due to breaking rules or regulations can be extremely detrimental to a person's or organization's capacity to conduct business.

4.3.9. **Increased Regulatory Review:** Repeated infractions may result in heightened regulatory review. This can result in the need for more frequent audits, inspections, and reporting.

4.3.10. **Civil and Criminal Records:** Legal repercussions may lead to the establishment of a criminal or civil record, which may have long-term repercussions on a person's personal and professional life.

To prevent these legal and regulatory repercussions, it is crucial for individuals and organizations to be informed of the rules and regulations that apply to their activities and to take the necessary precautions to assure compliance. Legal counsel and the implementation of strong compliance programs can assist reduce the risks posed by regulatory infractions.

4.4. The Human Cost

The human cost of a cyberattack refers to how the attack affects people individually and collectively. While cyber-attacks are frequently linked to technical and financial repercussions, they can also have important direct and indirect effects on people.

The human cost of a cyberattack may emerge in various ways, including the following:

4.4.1. **Financial Loss**: Cyberattacks can result in financial losses for both individuals and companies. People's financial security may be directly impacted by stolen money, fraud, and the expense of restoring networks and data.

4.4.2. **Identity Theft**: Through data breaches, cybercriminals may obtain personal information that results in identity theft. Financial difficulties, emotional discomfort, and the drawn-out process of dealing with identity theft issues are possible for victims.

4.4.3. **Emotional Distress:** Experiencing mental discomfort as a result of a cyberattack is common. Anxiety, despair, and stress can be brought on by privacy violations, the loss of personal information, and the worry of additional attacks.

4.4.4. **Loss of Privacy**: In the digital age, privacy is a major problem. Cyber-attacks have the potential to expose private and sensitive data, undermining people's feeling of privacy.

4.4.5. **Data Breaches:** In the event of a data breach, people's sensitive and private information, such as communications, financial information, and medical records, may be made public. This may result in exploitation, blackmail, or public humiliation.

4.4.6. **Disruption of Services:** Services can be disrupted as a result of cyberattacks against important infrastructure, such as hospitals or utilities. Particularly in healthcare settings, this can have potentially fatal results.

4.4.7. **Job Loss:** Companies that experience serious cyberattacks may be forced to downsize or close, which will result in job losses for staff. Unemployment can take a significant toll on one's finances and mental health.

4.4.8. **Cyberbullying:** In some circumstances, cyberattacks may target specific people or organizations with the aim of threatening, intimidating, or bullying them. In severe circumstances, cyberbullying can cause physical harm in addition to mental trauma.

4.4.9. **Loss of Trust**: Clients and customers may stop having faith in businesses after data breaches or other cyberattacks. Relationships and reputations may suffer long-term harm as a result of this.

4.4.10. **Public Safety:** Cyber assaults on vital infrastructure, transportation networks, or public safety organizations can jeopardize public safety and security and even cause hurt or fatalities.

4.4.11. **Secondary Effects:** Cyberattacks may have secondary repercussions that extend beyond the immediate victims to suppliers, customers, and communities. These incidental impacts may result in job losses, a broken supply chain, and financial difficulties.

4.4.12. **Increased Cybersecurity Measures:** To defend against cyberattacks, people and businesses may need to spend more money and time on their cybersecurity defences.

In order to reduce the technical and financial consequences of cyberattacks, it is also necessary to support and resource the impacted people and communities. This involves assisting victims, educating people about cybersecurity, and promoting improved cybersecurity procedures and laws. Strong cybersecurity policies and education are two preventive strategies that can assist lower the human cost of cyberattacks by lessening the likelihood and severity of those attacks.

Chapter 5: Mitigating Cybersecurity Risks

5.1. Developing a Comprehensive Cybersecurity Strategy

The following is a thorough overview of the procedures necessary in creating a thorough cybersecurity strategy:

1. **Recognize Your Company:** Get to know your company's activities, commercial goals, and the worth of its digital assets thoroughly to start. Determine the vital operations, systems, and data.
2. **Specify Specific Goals**: Set SMART (specific, measurable, attainable, relevant, and time-bound) cybersecurity goals that are in line with your corporate objectives. Your strategy should be determined by these goals.
3. **Determine Regulatory Conditions**: Find out whether industry rules, data protection laws, or compliance requirements (such GDPR, HIPAA, or PCI DSS) your company must follow. Make sure your plan complies with these demands.
4. **Carry Out A Risk Analysis:** To find potential risks, weaknesses, and the potential effects of security incidents on your firm, do a thorough risk assessment. Sort dangers according to their importance.
5. **Create security guidelines and practices:** Establish clear, thorough, and industry-aligned security policies, processes, and recommendations that address identified concerns.
6. **Distribute Resources:** Calculate the amount of money, personnel, and technology needed to successfully implement your cybersecurity strategy. Make sure you have the required resources, both financial and human.
7. **Put Security Controls In Place**: To reduce recognized threats, use a variety of security controls including firewalls,

intrusion detection systems, encryption, access controls, and antivirus software.

8. **Develop An Incident Response Strategy**: Create a thorough incident response strategy that outlines what to do in the event of a security breach. Roles, responsibilities, communication protocols, and recovery methods should all be part of this strategy.
9. **Promote a Culture of Security**: Encourage all staff members to be aware of cybersecurity issues. To inform personnel about security concerns and best practices, conduct frequent training sessions and awareness campaigns.
10. **Constant Testing and Monitoring**: Utilize tools and procedures like penetration testing, vulnerability scanning, and security information and event management (SIEM) systems to continuously monitor your security posture.
11. **Evaluation and Management of Vendors:** Examine the security procedures followed by partners and third-party vendors who have access to your systems or data. Make sure your security requirements are met.
12. **Data Encryption and Protection:** Sensitive data should be encrypted both in transit and at rest. To lessen the risk of data breaches, establish policies for data retention and destruction.
13. **Regular Patch Management and Updates:** To address known vulnerabilities, keep up with software updates, security patches, and firmware upgrades.
14. **Business Continuity and Disaster Recovery:** To make sure your company can recover from security incidents and sustain key activities, develop and test disaster recovery and business continuity strategies.
15. **Documenting and Reporting Incidents:** To report and record security occurrences, create a process. Make sure that every occurrence is thoroughly investigated and recorded for

review and improvement.

16. **Constant Development:** Review and revise your cybersecurity strategy on a regular basis in light of new threats, evolving business requirements, and findings from security assessments and incident response.
17. **Considerations for Legal and Compliance:** Make sure your cybersecurity approach conforms to all relevant rules and regulations by working closely with legal counsel.
18. **Communication and Involvement of Stakeholders**: Share your cybersecurity strategy with all relevant parties, including management, staff, clients, and partners. Encourage communication and cooperation among security personnel.
19. **Key Performance Indicators (KPIs) And Metrics:** Establish KPIs and metrics to assess the success of your cybersecurity plan. Review and report on your security posture on a regular basis.
20. **Executive and Board Reporting:** To keep the board and senior leadership informed and involved in security activities, provide cybersecurity updates and reports.
21. **Table-top Exercises and Incident Simulation**: Test the efficiency of your security measures and your incident response plan using simulated exercises.
22. **Reputation Management and Public Relations:** Prepare a reputation management and public relations strategy to handle any potential consequences of security events.

Always keep in mind that developing a thorough cybersecurity strategy is a continuous process. To effectively address new risks and safeguard the digital assets of your firm, you must continually adapt and evolve your strategy.

5.2. Security Policies and Procedures

The fundamental elements of any organization's comprehensive security strategy are security policies and procedures. They offer policies and procedures that aid in safeguarding an organization's resources, data, and assets against a variety of dangers, both internal and external.

I'll list a few crucial components of security procedures and policies below:

5.2.1. **Develop a Security Policy**: Establishing the organization's security needs and goals is the first step in developing security policy. Regulations and industry norms should be reflected in policies. The creation of policies frequently involves a cross-functional team made up of management, IT, legal, HR, and other departments.

5.2.2. **Documenting policies:** Policies should be succinctly and clearly documented. They must outline the objectives, parameters, roles, and procedures for enforcement. Data protection, access control, network security, and incident response are typical security policy issues.

5.2.3. **Access Control:** Access control procedures specify who has access to which organizational resources. User accounts, permissions, and authentication techniques like passwords, MFA, and biometrics are all included in this.

5.2.4. **Data Protection:** Data security rules specify the proper methods for handling, storing, and transmitting sensitive data. This covers data classification, data retention policies, and encryption requirements.

5.2.5. **Network Security:** Firewalls, intrusion detection and prevention systems, VPN usage, and remote access regulations are all covered by network security policies. These guarantee the privacy, reliability, and accessibility of network resources.

5.2.6. **Incident Response**: The organization's response to security issues like data breaches, malware infections, or illegal access is outlined in incident response protocols. They offer recommendations for incident reporting, containment, investigation, and communication.

5.2.7. **Physical Security:** Policies for protecting physical assets, such as servers, data centres, and infrastructure, are referred to as physical security. They include things like surveillance, visitor management, and access controls.

5.2.8. **Employee Security Awareness Training**: Policies should specify that staff must receive security awareness training. A vital line of protection against security risks is properly trained personnel.

5.2.9. **Compliance and Auditing:** The organization's security policies should guarantee that it conforms to all applicable laws, rules, and industry standards. Verifying policy conformity through regular audits and reviews.

5.2.10. **Review and Updates**: Policies and procedures should be reviewed and updated regularly. They must adapt to new threats and alterations in the organizational structure or technological environment. It's crucial to conduct regular reviews and updates.

5.2.11. **Enforcement and Repercussions:** Policies should specify the repercussions of breaking them. Depending on the seriousness of the infraction, enforcement measures may include warnings, suspension, termination, or legal action.

5.2.12. **Security of Third-Party Partners and Vendors:** If the organization depends on third-party partners or vendors, policies should cover how their security measures adhere to the company's standards.

5.2.13. **Disaster Recovery and Business Continuity:** These procedures make sure that the company can recover from security breaches or natural disasters while continuing to carry out its core duties.

5.2.14. **Incidents That Were Documented:** Policies ought to demand that every security event, every inquiry, and every course of action be documented. This aids in enhancing security posture and learning from previous instances.

5.2.15. **Communication Strategy**: Policies should outline how and when information about security events or breaches will be shared both internally and externally with clients, partners, and regulatory authorities.

Protecting an organization's assets and reputation requires effective security policies and processes. To handle new dangers and provide continued protection, they should be examined and updated on a regular basis. To foster a culture of security awareness among all employees, they should also be explained to and understood by everyone.

5.3. Employee Training and Awareness

Any organization's plan for preserving a successful and secure workplace must include essential elements like employee awareness and training. The significance of staff education and training will be discussed in this section, along with some crucial factors to take into account when putting in place successful programs:

5.3.1. Employee Education And Awareness Is Important:

a. **Cybersecurity:** Employees need to be aware of cybersecurity hazards and best practices in an increasingly digital world. Through training, they can spot phishing efforts, safeguard sensitive information, and stay safe online.

b. **Compliance.** Regulations and compliance requirements are stringent in many businesses. Training guarantees that staff members are aware of and abide by these rules, lowering the possibility of legal troubles and fines.

c. **Enhancement of Skills**: Ongoing training keeps staff members abreast of the newest developments in technology and the industry. This could enhance their abilities and increase their worth.

d. **Safety:** Appropriate training is crucial for employee safety in industries like manufacturing or healthcare. Accidents and injuries can be avoided by being aware of safety regulations and procedures.

e. **Productivity:** Employees with proper training perform their jobs more effectively and efficiently, which can increase overall productivity.

5.3.2. Key Points for Programs of Employee Awareness and Training:

a. **Assessment:** Begin by determining the precise training requirements for your firm. Determine the areas where employees can improve or where adherence to rules is essential.

b. **Customization:** Design training courses to meet the specific needs of your company. Generic training might not be as successful as material created specifically for your business and industry.

c. **Regular Updates:** Training should not be a one-time event but rather an ongoing activity. Update training materials frequently to reflect changes in technology, laws, and best practices.

d. **Engagement:** Include interactive elements in your training. To maintain employees' interest and aid with information retention, think about utilizing multimedia, quizzes, and simulations.

e. **Accessibility**: Ensure that all employees may easily access the training materials. Give remote or flexible workers internet options to choose from.

f. **Feedback and Evaluation**: Obtain employee opinions regarding the training initiatives. Utilize this information to inform improvements and gauge the training's efficacy.

g. **Employer Training and Awareness Initiatives**: Must have the active support and encouragement of managers and supervisors. Success depends on getting their support.

h. **Incentives:** Offering incentives or awards for finishing training courses or hitting certain milestones is something to think about. This may encourage workers to actively participate.

i. **Documentation:** Keep track of the staff education and awareness campaigns. For audits, compliance checks, and performance reviews, this paperwork may be useful.

j. **Culture of Learning:** Encourage an environment where learning is ongoing inside the company. Encourage staff members to take responsibility for their own progress and look for opportunities to do so.

In conclusion, employee education and awareness are crucial to the security and prosperity of a company. Businesses can increase the skills of their personnel, lower risks, and keep a competitive advantage in today's dynamic business environment by investing in these initiatives and remaining dedicated to continual improvement.

5.4. Security Tools and Technologies

A strong cybersecurity plan must include security tools and technologies. They assist firms in safeguarding their digital assets, identifying risks, and successfully handling security incidents. We will explore a variety of security tools and technologies that are frequently utilized in the cybersecurity scene in this section:

5.4.1. **Firewalls:** Network security tools known as firewalls monitor and filter incoming and outgoing network traffic in accordance with specified security policies. They aid in preventing illegal access and offer protection from numerous online dangers.

5.4.1. **Antivirus Software:** Software for detecting and removing viruses, Trojan horses, and other dangerous applications. Antivirus software searches files and programs for known malware signatures and behaviour patterns.

5.4.2. **Intrusion Detection Systems (IDS) and Intrusion Prevention Systems (IPS):** IDS and IPS solutions scan network traffic for unusual activity or well-known attack patterns. These systems detect and prevent intrusions. While IPS can actively block or mitigate threats in real-time, IDS can notify administrators to prospective dangers.

5.4.3. **Security Information and Event Management (SIEM) Systems:** SIEM systems, also known as security information and event management systems, gather and analyse log data from a variety of sources, such as network devices, servers, and apps, in order to identify and look into security issues.

5.4.4. **Endpoint Security Solutions:** These solutions safeguard particular gadgets, or endpoints, such laptops and smartphones. They consist of endpoint detection and response (EDR) tools, antivirus, and anti-malware programs.

5.4.5. **Tools for Encryption:** Both data in transit and data at rest are protected using encryption technologies. This includes file encryption, full-disk encryption, and secure communication protocols (like HTTPS).

5.4.6. **Solutions for Identity and Access Management (IAM)**: IAM tools are used to control user identities, access rights, and authentication procedures. They make sure that only individuals with permission can access resources and data.

5.4.7. **Multi-Factor Authentication (MFA)**: MFA adds an additional layer of protection by asking users to enter various forms of identification (such as a password, fingerprint, or token) in order to access a system or account.

5.4.8. **Network Security Scanners**: These devices check for holes and incorrect setups in networks and systems. They offer reports that assist enterprises in prioritizing and fixing security problems.

5.4.9. **Solutions for Data Loss Prevention (DLP)**: In order to stop illegal access or data leakage, DLP solutions monitor and safeguard critical data. They can also assist firms in adhering to data privacy laws.

5.4.10. **Web application firewalls (WAF):** WAFs shield web applications from common security risks including SQL injection, cross-site scripting (XSS), and other attack types that target the application layer.

5.4.11. **Solutions for Security Orchestration, Automation, and Response (SOAR):** SOAR solutions automate workflows for responding to security issues, allowing for a quicker and more effective response.

5.4.12. **Virtual Private Networks (VPNs):** VPNs build private communication tunnels over open networks to protect the confidentiality and integrity of data.

5.4.13. **Tools for Security knowledge and Training:** Through training modules and simulations, these tools assist firms in educating staff about cybersecurity best practices and gauging their knowledge.

5.4.14. **Tools for Penetration Testing**: These tools imitate cyberattacks in order to find security flaws and vulnerabilities within an organization.

5.4.15. **Cloud Security Solutions**: These are being adopted by more businesses as they migrate to the cloud to protect their data, applications, and infrastructure.

5.4.16. **Behavioural Analytics and User Behaviour Monitoring**: These techniques, known as behavioural analytics and user behaviour monitoring, examine user behaviour in order to spot irregularities and possible insider threats based on deviations from the norm.

5.4.17. **Threat Intelligence Platforms:** Platforms for gathering and analysing data on new threats and vulnerabilities are known as threat intelligence platforms, and they assist enterprises in staying informed and proactive with regard to security measures.

5.4.18. **Mobile Security and Mobile Device Management (MDM):** MDM solutions control and safeguard employee-owned mobile devices to ensure they abide by security regulations.

5.4.19. **Tools for Security knowledge and Training:** Through training modules and simulations, these tools assist firms in educating staff about cybersecurity best practices and gauging their knowledge.

Chapter 6: Antivirus and Endpoint Protection

Security solutions like antivirus and endpoint protection are made to defend networks and computer systems from numerous threats like malware, viruses, ransomware, and other harmful actions. Here is a quick synopsis of each:

1. **Antivirus Programs**: Security software's core element is antivirus protection. Its main objective is to locate and eliminate known viruses and malware from a computer or network. Important features include real-time application and file scanning, frequent system scans, and automated virus definition updates to stay up to date with emerging threats. The signature-based detection method used by antivirus software involves comparing files and code to a database of known malware signatures. The antivirus program takes action to quarantine or eliminate the danger if a match is discovered. Antivirus software, also known as anti-malware software, is designed to detect, prevent, and remove malicious software from a computer or network.

Here are some key features and functions of antivirus software:

a. **Scanning:** Antivirus software regularly scans files, programs, and the entire system for known patterns or signatures of malware. It compares files and processes against a database of known threats.
b. **Real-time Protection:** Most modern antivirus programs offer real-time protection, which monitors system activities and incoming data in real-time. If it detects suspicious behaviour or files, it can block or quarantine them

immediately.

c. **Automatic Updates:** Antivirus software frequently updates its signature database to stay current with new malware threats. This ensures that the software can recognize and protect against the latest threats.
d. **Quarantine and Remediation:** When a potential threat is detected, antivirus software often quarantines the suspicious file or program, preventing it from executing. Users can then review and take appropriate action, such as deleting or restoring the file.
e. **Scheduled Scans:** Users can schedule regular system scans to ensure ongoing protection against malware. These scans can be daily, weekly, or at other intervals based on user preferences.

1. **Endpoint Security**: Endpoint security, commonly referred to as endpoint protection, is a more comprehensive and sophisticated method of cybersecurity that goes beyond conventional antivirus software. It includes a variety of security methods to safeguard endpoints, which are standalone devices connected to a network including computers, cell phones, and tablets. Antivirus, firewall, intrusion detection and prevention, behaviour analysis, application whitelisting, and data loss prevention are common characteristics found in endpoint protection solutions. Modern endpoint security solutions, in contrast to classical antivirus, use heuristic analysis and machine learning algorithms to identify and address emerging and unidentified threats. Endpoint protection is especially useful in corporate settings since it helps safeguard several devices on a network within a company.

Endpoint security is a broader concept that encompasses various security measures and solutions designed to protect the endpoints in a network. Endpoints include devices such as desktops, laptops, smartphones, and tablets.

Here are some key aspects of endpoint security:

a. **Antivirus as Part of Endpoint Security:** Antivirus software is a fundamental component of endpoint security. However, endpoint security solutions go beyond antivirus by integrating other security layers.
b. **Firewalls:** Endpoint security solutions often include firewalls that monitor and control network traffic, preventing unauthorized access and blocking malicious incoming and outgoing connections.
c. **Intrusion Detection and Prevention (IDS/IPS):** These systems monitor network traffic for suspicious activities and can block or alert administrators to potential threats.
d. **Device Management:** Endpoint security solutions often include device management features, allowing administrators to enforce security policies, apply updates, and remotely wipe or lock devices in case of loss or theft.
e. **Data Encryption:** Protecting sensitive data is critical, and endpoint security can include data encryption capabilities to secure data at rest and during transmission.
f. **Behavioural Analysis:** Some advanced endpoint security solutions use behavioural analysis to detect and respond to unknown threats based on suspicious behaviour patterns, rather than relying solely on known signatures.
g. **Security Patch Management:** Keeping operating systems and software up to date is crucial. Endpoint security solutions can help manage patching and updates to reduce vulnerabilities.

Antivirus software finds and fights malware. Endpoint security protects all network endpoints with many methods. A comprehensive cybersecurity strategy needs both components to safeguard systems and data. Thus, antivirus software is a key tool for finding and eliminating known malware, whereas endpoint protection adopts a more thorough strategy, integrating a variety of security features to protect against a wider range of threats, such as zero-day attacks and advanced persistent threats. Both are crucial elements of a multi-layered cybersecurity approach to shield computers and networks from the constantly changing threats of the modern internet.

6.1 The Role of Antivirus Software

Antivirus software plays a critical role in cybersecurity by shielding computer systems and networks from a variety of malware and nefarious attacks. The following are the main jobs and duties of antivirus software:

6.1.1 **Malware Detection:** The main function of antivirus software is to find and classify different kinds of malware, such as viruses, worms, Trojan horses, spyware, adware, and ransomware. It accomplishes this by comparing computer files and applications to a database of recognized malware signatures.

6.1.2 **Real-Time Scanning**: Antivirus software offers real-time security by continuously keeping track of all files, processes, and events occurring on a computer or network. It takes steps to stop or quarantine any unusual activity or files that match well-known malware signatures.

6.1.3 **Behavioural Analysis:** Some advanced antivirus solutions employ behavioural analysis techniques. They detect suspicious or malicious activities by analysing the behaviour of programs and processes, instead of just using known malware signatures. This helps in identifying previously unknown threats.

6.1.4 **Automatic Updates:** To effectively combat evolving malware threats, antivirus software regularly updates its signature database. These updates ensure that the software can recognize and block the latest malware variants and attack techniques.

6.1.5 **Quarantine and Remediation:** Antivirus software stops potential threats by keeping them in quarantine. Users can then review and take appropriate action, such as deleting or restoring the file.

6.1.6 **Scheduled Scans:** Antivirus software allows users to schedule regular system scans. These scans can be performed daily, weekly, or at other intervals, based on user preferences. Scheduled scans help ensure ongoing protection against malware.

6.1.7 **Email and Web Protection:** Many antivirus solutions include email and web protection features. They scan email attachments and web content for malicious links and attachments, reducing the risk of phishing attacks and malware downloads.

6.1.8 **Firewall Integration:** Some antivirus software packages integrate with firewalls to provide a more comprehensive security solution. This combination helps in monitoring and controlling incoming and outgoing network traffic.

6.1.9 **Reporting and Alerts:** Antivirus software often generates reports and alerts to keep users and administrators informed about security threats, scan results, and system status. This helps in proactive threat mitigation.

6.1.10 **User-Friendly Interface:** Antivirus software typically comes with a user-friendly interface that allows users to easily configure settings, initiate scans, and view reports. Usability is important to ensure that users can effectively manage their security.

6.1.11 **Compatibility:** Antivirus software should be compatible with the operating systems and software applications used in your environment. Compatibility issues can lead to gaps in security.

6.1.12 **Low Resource Usage:** Effective antivirus software should be resource-efficient, minimizing the impact on system performance. This ensures that the protection doesn't slow down the computer.

In summary, antivirus software plays a vital role in preventing and mitigating malware threats. It serves as a frontline defence mechanism by detecting and blocking malicious software, offering real-time protection, and continuously updating its knowledge base to combat evolving threats. While antivirus software is an essential component of cybersecurity, it is often used in conjunction with other security measures, such as firewalls, intrusion detection systems, and user education, to provide comprehensive protection against a wide range of threats.

6.2 Choosing the Right Antivirus Solution

Choosing the right antivirus solution is a critical decision for ensuring the security of your computer or network. Here are some essential factors and considerations to keep in mind when selecting an antivirus solution:

6.2.1 **Security Effectiveness:** Look for antivirus software that has a high detection rate for known malware and can effectively detect and block emerging threats. Independent antivirus testing organizations can provide insight into the effectiveness of different products.

6.2.2 **Real-Time Protection:** Ensure the antivirus solution offers real-time scanning and protection. It should continuously monitor your system and incoming data for threats and promptly respond to them.

6.2.3 **Resource Usage:** Antivirus software should be resource-efficient, meaning it should not significantly slow down your computer's performance. Consider how the antivirus affects system performance, especially if you have older hardware.

6.2.4 **Compatibility:** Verify that the antivirus solution is compatible with your operating system and other software applications. Some antivirus programs may have specific requirements or conflicts with certain software.

6.2.5 **Ease of Use:** Choose antivirus software that has a user-friendly interface and is easy to configure. It should provide clear instructions for actions like scans and updates.

6.2.6 **Automatic Updates:** Regular updates are essential to keep the antivirus software's virus definitions and detection capabilities up-to-date. Ensure that the antivirus program offers automatic updates.

6.2.7 **Scanning Options:** Consider your scanning needs. Look for software that offers various scanning options, including quick scans, full system scans, and custom scans that allow you to scan specific folders or files.

6.2.8 **Quarantine and Remediation:** The antivirus software should have a robust quarantine system for isolating and managing detected threats. It should also provide guidance on how to remediate or remove threats safely.

6.2.9 **Customer Support:** Evaluate the level of customer support and technical assistance offered by the antivirus provider. Responsive customer support can be crucial if you encounter issues or have questions.

6.2.10 **Additional Features:** Some antivirus solutions include extra features like firewalls, VPNs, password managers, and identity theft protection. Consider whether these additional features align with your security needs.

6.2.11 **Price and Licensing:** Antivirus software comes in both free and paid versions. Assess your budget and the specific features you need when choosing between free and paid options. Paid versions often provide more comprehensive protection.

6.2.12 **Reviews and Recommendations:** Read reviews and seek recommendations from trusted sources, such as cybersecurity experts, online forums, and colleagues who have experience with antivirus software.

6.2.13 **Business vs. Home Use:** If you're choosing antivirus for a business environment, consider solutions that offer centralized management, reporting, and scalability to meet the organization's security needs.

6.2.14 **Privacy Considerations:** Be aware of the privacy policies of the antivirus provider. Some antivirus software may collect data about your activities for various purposes, so make sure you're comfortable with their data usage practices.

6.2.15 **Trial Period:** Whenever possible, take advantage of free trials to test the antivirus software in your specific environment before making a long-term commitment.

Remember that the best antivirus solution may vary depending on your individual or organizational needs. Take the time to research and compare options to find the one that provides the best balance of security, performance, and features for your specific requirements.

6.3 Best Practices for Endpoint Security

Implementing strong endpoint security is essential for protecting your organization's devices and data from various cyber threats. Here are some best practices for effective endpoint security:

6.3.1 **Use Antivirus and Antimalware Software:** Deploy reputable antivirus and antimalware software on all endpoint devices. Keep the software updated to ensure it can detect and mitigate the latest threats.

6.3.2 **Regular Software Updates and Patch Management:** Ensure that operating systems, applications, and firmware on all endpoint devices are regularly updated with security patches. Attackers often exploit vulnerabilities in outdated software.

6.3.3 **Network Segmentation:** Segment your network to limit lateral movement for attackers. Separate sensitive data and systems from less critical ones using firewalls and access controls.

6.3.4 **Implement Strong Authentication:** Enforce the use of strong, multi-factor authentication (MFA) for access to sensitive systems and data. This adds an extra layer of security beyond passwords.

6.3.5 **Endpoint Detection and Response (EDR):** Invest in EDR solutions that provide real-time monitoring and response capabilities. These systems can help detect and mitigate advanced threats.

6.3.6 **Data Encryption:** Encrypt data at rest and in transit to protect it from unauthorized access. Use encryption protocols like TLS/SSL for network traffic and full-disk encryption for devices.

6.3.7 **User Training and Awareness:** Educate employees about security best practices, such as recognizing phishing emails, avoiding suspicious downloads, and reporting security incidents promptly.

6.3.8 **Application Whitelisting:** Implement application whitelisting to only allow approved applications to run on endpoint devices. This prevents unauthorized or malicious software from executing.

6.3.9 **Regular Backups:** Perform regular backups of critical data and systems. Ensure backups are stored securely and can be restored quickly in case of a ransomware attack or data loss.

6.3.10 **Mobile Device Management (MDM):** Use MDM solutions to manage and secure mobile devices used within your organization. This includes enforcing security policies, remote wiping capabilities, and app management.

6.3.11 **Incident Response Plan:** Develop and regularly update an incident response plan. Ensure that employees know how to respond to security incidents and have designated roles and responsibilities.

6.3.12 **Endpoint Security Policies:** Create and enforce clear security policies for endpoint devices. Define acceptable use, password requirements, and other security guidelines.

6.3.13 **Remote Work Security:** Extend endpoint security practices to remote and mobile devices. Use VPNs and secure remote access solutions to protect data when employees work outside the office.

6.3.14 **Access Control and Least Privilege:** Limit user access to only the resources and data necessary for their roles. Apply the principle of least privilege to reduce the attack surface.

6.3.15 **Security Auditing and Monitoring:** Continuously monitor and audit endpoint devices and network traffic for suspicious activities. Use log analysis tools to detect anomalies.

6.3.16 **Regular Security Assessments:** Conduct regular security assessments, including penetration testing and vulnerability scanning, to identify and address weaknesses in your endpoint security.

6.3.17 **Vendor and Third-Party Risk Assessment:** Assess the security of third-party applications and services that interact with your endpoint devices. Ensure they meet your security standards.

6.3.18 **Incident Reporting and Response Testing:** Periodically test your incident response plan through simulated exercises. Ensure that your team can effectively respond to security incidents.

6.3.19 **Compliance with Regulations:** Stay informed about cybersecurity regulations and standards that may apply to your organization. Ensure compliance with data protection laws and industry-specific requirements.

6.3.20 **Regular Security Training and Updates:** Stay up-to-date with the latest cybersecurity threats and best practices by attending training sessions, webinars, and subscribing to security newsletters.

Effective endpoint security requires a combination of technology, policies, and user awareness. By implementing these best practices, you can significantly reduce the risk of security breaches and protect your organization's valuable assets.

6.4. Key Components in the Modern Cybersecurity Landscape:

Component	Description
Firewalls	Network security devices that filter incoming and outgoing traffic based on predefined security rules.
Intrusion Detection System (IDS)	Monitors network traffic for signs of malicious activities or security breaches.
Intrusion Prevention System (IPS)	Goes a step further than IDS by actively blocking or preventing suspicious activities.
Antivirus/Antimalware	Software designed to detect, prevent, and remove malware infections from endpoints and networks.
VPN (Virtual Private Network)	Securely connects remote users or networks to private networks over the internet.
Encryption	The process of converting data into a code to prevent unauthorized access, data breaches, or eavesdropping.
Two-Factor Authentication (2FA)	Enhances login security by requiring users to provide two different authentication factors.
Endpoint Security	Protects individual devices (endpoints) from threats, including antivirus, firewall, and threat detection
Web Application Firewall	Protects web applications from various web-based threats such as SQL injection and cross-site scripting (XSS).
SIEM (Security Information and Event Management)	Collects and analyses log data for security monitoring and incident response.
Access Control	Enforces policies that determine who can access specific resources and what actions they can perform
Security Awareness Training	Provides cybersecurity education to employees to mitigate the risk of social engineering attacks.
Patch Management	Ensures software and systems are up-to-date with the latest security patches and updates.
Disaster Recovery and Business Continuity	Plans and strategies to maintain business operations in the event of a cyber incident.

Network Segmentation	Divides a network into smaller segments to contain and isolate potential security breaches.
Mobile Device Management (MDM)	Controls and secures mobile devices used within an organization, often including remote wipe capabilities
Cloud Security	Security measures and policies designed to protect data and applications hosted in cloud environments.
Incident Response Plan	A documented plan outlining steps to follow when a cybersecurity incident occurs, aiding swift recovery.
Threat Intelligence	Information about the latest threats and vulnerabilities used to enhance cybersecurity measures.
Penetration Testing	Ethical hacking tests to identify vulnerabilities and weaknesses in an organization's security defences.

Copyright: Patrick Mukosha (2023), Computer Viruses Unveiled: *Types, Trends and Mitigation Strategies.*

Figure 3: Key Components in the Modern Cybersecurity Landscape

Note: This table provides a high-level overview of some of the key components in the modern cybersecurity landscape. In practice, organizations may have more specific and tailored security measures based on their needs and risk profiles. The effectiveness of cybersecurity depends on a combination of these components working together in a cohesive strategy.

Chapter 7: Network Security

7.1 Understanding Network Security

Network security is a critical aspect of cybersecurity that focuses on protecting the integrity, confidentiality, and availability of data and resources within a computer network. It involves a combination of technologies, policies, and practices designed to defend against a wide range of threats and vulnerabilities that can compromise network systems and the information they contain.

Here are key aspects and considerations related to network security:

7.1.1 **Types of Threats:** Network security addresses various types of threats, including malware (viruses, worms, Trojans), ransomware, phishing attacks, Distributed Denial of Service (DDoS) attacks, unauthorized access, insider threats, and data breaches.

7.1.2 **Security Layers:** Network security typically employs multiple layers of defence, often referred to as defence in depth. These layers include perimeter security (firewalls), intrusion detection and prevention systems (IDS/IPS), network segmentation, and endpoint security.

7.1.3 **Firewalls:** Firewalls act as gatekeepers between a trusted internal network and untrusted external networks (e.g., the internet). They control incoming and outgoing traffic based on a set of predefined rules and policies, blocking unauthorized access and potentially malicious content.

7.1.4 **Intrusion Detection and Prevention Systems (IDS/IPS):** IDS/IPS systems monitor network traffic for suspicious patterns or activities. IDS identifies potential threats and generates alerts, while IPS can actively block or mitigate identified threats.

7.1.5 **Encryption:** Data encryption (e.g., TLS/SSL) ensures that data transmitted over the network is secure and cannot be intercepted or tampered with by unauthorized entities.

7.1.6 **Access Control:** Access control mechanisms, such as authentication and authorization, ensure that only authorized users and devices have access to specific network resources. Multi-factor authentication (MFA) adds an extra layer of security.

7.1.7 **Network Segmentation:** Segmentation divides a network into smaller, isolated segments to limit the potential impact of a security breach. It helps contain threats and prevents lateral movement by attackers.

7.1.8 **Vulnerability Management:** Regularly scanning for and patching known vulnerabilities in network devices, servers, and applications is crucial to reduce the risk of exploitation.

7.1.9 **Security Policies:** Clearly defined network security policies outline rules and procedures for users and administrators, specifying acceptable use, password policies, and incident response procedures.

7.1.10 **Monitoring and Logging:** Continuous monitoring of network traffic and activity, along with comprehensive logging, helps detect suspicious behaviour and provides data for forensic analysis in case of security incidents.

7.1.11 **Intrusion Detection and Incident Response:** Having an effective incident detection and response plan in place is critical. This includes identifying, containing, and mitigating security incidents and learning from them to improve security posture.

7.1.12 **Security Awareness and Training:** Educating employees and users about security best practices, social engineering tactics, and how to recognize and report security threats is essential in preventing human-related security breaches.

7.1.13 **Mobile Device and Remote Access Security:** As remote work becomes more common, securing mobile devices and remote access to the network is crucial. Mobile device management (MDM) and Virtual Private Networks (VPNs) are used for this purpose.

7.1.14 **Regular Security Audits and Penetration Testing:** Periodic security assessments, including penetration testing and vulnerability scanning, help identify weaknesses in the network and validate the effectiveness of security measures.

7.1.15 **Compliance with Regulations:** Ensure that network security practices comply with industry-specific regulations and data protection laws, such as GDPR, HIPAA, and PCI DSS, where applicable.

7.1.16 **Backup and Disaster Recovery:** Regularly back up critical data and have a robust disaster recovery plan in place to ensure data availability and business continuity in the event of a breach or system failure.

Network security is an ongoing process that requires vigilance and adaptability to address evolving threats. A comprehensive network security strategy is essential for organizations to protect their digital assets and maintain the trust of their customers and stakeholders.

7.2 Firewalls and Intrusion Detection Systems (IDS)

Firewalls and Intrusion Detection Systems (IDS) are critical components of network security. They serve distinct but complementary roles in safeguarding computer networks from unauthorized access and potential threats. Let's delve into each of them in more detail:

7.2.1. Firewalls:

a. **Role of Firewalls:** Firewalls act as a barrier between an internal network (e.g., a corporate LAN) and external networks (e.g., the internet). Their primary role is to filter and control the flow of network traffic based on a set of predetermined rules and policies.
b. **Types of Firewalls:** There are several types of firewalls, including:
    - **Packet Filtering Firewalls:** These examine individual packets of data and make decisions to allow or block them based on defined rules.
    - **Stateful Inspection Firewalls:** They keep track of the state of active connections and make decisions based on the context of the traffic.
    - **Proxy Firewalls:** These act as intermediaries between internal and external networks, forwarding traffic on behalf of internal users.
    - **Next-Generation Firewalls (NGFWs):** NGFWs combine traditional firewall features with advanced capabilities, such as intrusion prevention, application-level filtering, and deep packet inspection.
c. **Functions of Firewalls:** Firewalls perform several functions,

including:

- **Packet Filtering:** They inspect packets of data and make decisions based on source and destination IP addresses, port numbers, and protocol types.
- **Access Control:** Firewalls enforce access control policies to determine which users or devices are allowed or denied access to specific resources.
- **Network Address Translation (NAT):** NAT is often used in firewalls to hide internal IP addresses from external networks, providing an additional layer of security.
- **Application Layer Filtering:** Some firewalls can inspect traffic at the application layer and block or allow specific applications or services.

d. **Benefits of Firewalls:** Firewalls provide essential network security benefits, such as:

- Protecting against unauthorized access and cyberattacks.
- Filtering out malicious traffic and known threats.
- Enforcing network segmentation to limit lateral movement for attackers.
- Logging and auditing network traffic for security analysis.

7.2.2. Intrusion Detection Systems (IDS):

a. **Role of IDS:** Intrusion Detection Systems (IDS) are designed to monitor network traffic and systems for signs of suspicious or malicious activity. Their primary role is to identify security incidents and generate alerts.

b. **Types of IDS:** There are two primary types of IDS:

- **Network-Based IDS (NIDS):** These IDS sensors monitor network traffic, looking for patterns or anomalies that indicate potential intrusions.

- **Host-Based IDS (HIDS):** HIDS agents are installed on individual hosts (servers or endpoints) and monitor activity on those hosts, including file changes and system log entries.

c. **Functions of IDS:** IDS systems perform the following functions:

- **Packet Inspection:** NIDS analyse network packets for known attack signatures or deviations from normal network behaviour.
- **Log Analysis:** HIDS review system logs, application logs, and event logs for signs of intrusion or abnormal activity.
- **Alert Generation:** When an IDS detects suspicious activity, it generates alerts, which can be sent to administrators for further investigation.

d. **Benefits of IDS:** IDS systems offer several advantages:

- Early Detection: They can identify potential threats and intrusions before they escalate into full-blown attacks.
- Threat Intelligence: IDS can provide valuable insights into emerging threats and attack patterns.
- Incident Response: By alerting administrators to security incidents, IDS helps facilitate a rapid response to mitigate the impact.

e. **Challenges:** IDS systems can generate a high volume of alerts, some of which may be false positives. Effective management and tuning are essential to reduce alert fatigue.

In summary, firewalls serve as the first line of defence by controlling network traffic and enforcing access policies, while Intrusion Detection Systems (IDS) continuously monitor for signs of malicious activity within the network. By combining the two, organizations can significantly enhance their network security posture, helping to protect against unauthorized access, cyberattacks, and potential breaches.

7.3 Virtual Private Networks (VPNs)

Virtual Private Networks (VPNs) are essential tools in the realm of network security and privacy. They provide a secure and encrypted tunnel for data transmission over public networks, allowing users to access resources and communicate securely while protecting their privacy. Here's an overview of VPNs, their functions, and their significance in the context of network security:

7.3.1. What is a VPN? A VPN is a technology that creates a secure, encrypted connection, often referred to as a tunnel, between a user's device (such as a computer, smartphone, or tablet) and a remote server or network. This connection passes through the public internet or another untrusted network.

7.3.2. How VPNs Work: When a user connects to a VPN, their internet traffic is routed through an encrypted tunnel to a VPN server. The VPN server acts as an intermediary, making it appear as if the user's connection is originating from the server's location rather than the user's physical location. This provides several benefits:

7.3.2.1. Security: VPNs encrypt data, making it extremely difficult for malicious actors to intercept or eavesdrop on the transmitted information. This is crucial for protecting sensitive data, especially when using public Wi-Fi networks.

7.3.2.2. Privacy: VPNs mask the user's IP address, enhancing online privacy by making it difficult for websites, advertisers, or ISPs to track their online activities.

7.3.2.3. Access to Restricted Content: VPNs can enable users to access regionally restricted or censored content by making it appear as if they are browsing from a different location.

7.4. Types of VPNs: There are several types of VPNs, including:

7.4.1. Remote Access VPNs: These allow individual users or remote workers to connect securely to a corporate network from outside locations.

7.4.2. Site-to-Site VPNs: These establish secure connections between multiple physical locations, such as branch offices, data centres, or partner networks.

7.4.3. SSL VPNs: These provide secure remote access to web applications and services through a web browser, without requiring the installation of dedicated VPN client software.

7.4.4. P2P VPNs: Peer-to-peer VPNs, often used in privacy-focused applications, enable users to create direct connections with one another for secure data sharing.

7.5. Benefits of VPNs: VPNs offer several advantages in terms of network security and privacy:

7.5.1. Encryption: VPNs encrypt data, making it unreadable to unauthorized parties. This is particularly important when transmitting sensitive information or accessing public Wi-Fi networks.

7.5.2. Bypassing Geographical Restrictions: VPNs allow users to access content and services that may be restricted or unavailable in their geographic location.

7.5.3. Enhanced Privacy: VPNs hide the user's IP address and online activities from prying eyes, including ISPs and potential trackers.

7.5.4. Security for Remote Work: In the era of remote work, VPNs provide a secure means for employees to access company resources and data from outside the corporate network.

7.5.5. Protection Against Network Snooping: VPNs protect against passive network monitoring and data interception, which can be employed by cybercriminals or governments.

7.6. Challenges and Considerations: While VPNs provide strong security and privacy benefits, it's essential to consider the following:

7.6.1. VPN Trustworthiness: Not all VPN services are equal. Users should choose reputable VPN providers with a strong commitment to privacy and a transparent privacy policy.

7.6.2. Impact on Connection Speed: VPNs can introduce latency and potentially reduce connection speed due to the encryption and routing processes. High-quality VPN providers aim to minimize this impact.

7.6.3. Logging Policies: Be aware of VPN providers that log user activity. Ideally, choose a VPN service with a strict no-logs policy.

7.6.4. Legal and Regulatory Compliance: Ensure that using a VPN complies with local laws and regulations in your jurisdiction.

Thus, VPNs are valuable tools for enhancing network security and privacy. They provide encryption, anonymity, and the ability to access restricted content, making them essential for users seeking to protect their online activities and sensitive data, especially in an era of remote work and growing privacy concerns. However, it's essential to choose a trustworthy VPN provider and be aware of potential limitations and legal considerations.

7.4 Network Segmentation

Network segmentation is a network security strategy that involves dividing a computer network into smaller, isolated segments or subnetworks to enhance security and reduce the risk of lateral movement for attackers. This practice is particularly valuable in protecting sensitive data, systems, and critical assets. Here's a closer look at network segmentation, its benefits, and implementation considerations:

7.4.1. Key Concepts and Principles:

7.4.1.1. Segmentation Zones: In a segmented network, each segment is often referred to as a "zone." Zones can be defined based on various criteria, such as department, function, security requirements, or trust levels.

7.4.1.2. Access Control: Network segmentation relies on strict access control policies and rules to determine who or what is allowed to communicate between different segments. Firewalls and routers are commonly used to enforce these policies.

7.4.1.3. Firewalls: Firewalls are a critical component of network segmentation. They act as gatekeepers between segments, controlling traffic flow based on predefined rules and policies. Next-generation firewalls (NGFWs) offer advanced capabilities, such as deep packet inspection and application-level filtering.

7.4.1.4. DMZ (Demilitarized Zone): Many networks include a DMZ, which is an intermediary segment between the internal network and the untrusted external network, typically the internet. The DMZ contains publicly accessible services like web servers or email servers, which are isolated from the internal network.

7.4.2. Benefits of Network Segmentation:

7.4.2.1. Enhanced Security: Network segmentation limits the attack surface by containing threats within isolated segments. If an attacker gains access to one segment, they may find it difficult to move laterally to other parts of the network.

7.4.2.2. Data Protection: Sensitive data can be stored in separate segments with stricter access controls, reducing the risk of unauthorized access or data breaches.

7.4.2.3. Reduced Impact of Compromises: In the event of a security breach, the impact is confined to the compromised segment, minimizing damage to the overall network.

7.4.2.4. Better Compliance: Network segmentation can help organizations meet regulatory compliance requirements by isolating and securing data that falls under specific compliance regulations.

7.4.2.5. Improved Performance and Traffic Management: By dividing the network into segments, organizations can optimize network performance and allocate resources more effectively to meet the needs of specific applications or user groups.

7.4.3. Considerations for Implementing Network Segmentation:

7.4.3.1. Segmentation Strategy: Define clear segmentation strategies based on the organization's security needs, business requirements, and data classification. Consider which assets need to be isolated and which need to communicate with each other.

7.4.3.2. Access Control Policies: Develop robust access control policies and firewall rules to govern traffic flow between segments. Ensure that only authorized traffic is allowed and that all other traffic is blocked by default.

7.4.3.3. DMZ Configuration: If you have publicly accessible services, configure your DMZ with additional security measures, such as web application firewalls (WAFs) and intrusion detection systems (IDS/IPS).

7.4.3.4. Monitoring and Logging: Implement network monitoring and logging tools to continuously monitor traffic and detect unusual or suspicious activity within each segment.

7.4.3.5. Regular Auditing and Testing: Periodically audit and test your network segmentation to ensure it aligns with your security policies and remains effective against evolving threats.

7.4.3.6. Security Updates and Patch Management: Keep all network devices, including firewalls and routers, up to date with the latest security patches and updates to mitigate vulnerabilities.

7.4.3.7. Employee Training: Educate employees about the importance of network segmentation and security best practices to prevent social engineering attacks that might compromise network integrity.

7.4.3.8. Documentation: Maintain documentation that outlines network segmentation policies, rules, and configurations for reference and auditing purposes.

Network segmentation is a proactive security measure that plays a crucial role in protecting against cyber threats and data breaches. By isolating critical assets and enforcing strict access controls, organizations can significantly enhance their overall network security posture.

7.5 Security Audits and Penetration Testing

Security audits and penetration testing (pen testing) are essential components of a comprehensive cybersecurity strategy. They help organizations identify vulnerabilities, assess security controls, and evaluate the effectiveness of their security measures. Here's an overview of security audits and penetration testing, their purposes, and how they differ:

7.5.1. Security Audits:

7.5.1.1. Purpose: Security audits are systematic assessments of an organization's information security policies, procedures, practices, and controls. The primary purpose is to ensure compliance with security policies, industry regulations, and best practices.

7.5.1.2. Types of Audits: There are various types of security audits, including:

- **Compliance Audits:** These focus on verifying that an organization adheres to specific regulatory or industry standards, such as GDPR, HIPAA, or ISO 27001.
- **Risk Assessments:** Risk audits evaluate an organization's overall security posture, identifying vulnerabilities and threats to assess the level of risk.
- **Internal Audits:** Conducted by an organization's internal audit team, these assess the effectiveness of internal controls and adherence to security policies.
- **Third-Party Audits:** External audit firms or certification bodies may perform audits to validate an organization's compliance with specific standards or regulations.

1. **Key Activities:** During a security audit, auditors typically perform the following activities:

- Review security policies, procedures, and documentation.
- Evaluate the implementation of security controls.
- Assess compliance with relevant standards and regulations.
- Conduct interviews and collect evidence.
- Generate audit reports with findings and recommendations.
    1. **Benefits:** Security audits help organizations:

- Ensure compliance with legal and regulatory requirements.
- Identify and address security weaknesses.
- Improve overall security governance.

Enhance the organization's reputation and trustworthiness.

7.5.4. Penetration Testing (Pen Testing):

7.5.4.1. Purpose: Penetration testing, often referred to as pen testing or ethical hacking, is a proactive security assessment that simulates real-world cyberattacks to identify vulnerabilities and weaknesses in an organization's systems, applications, and networks.

7.5.5. Types of Pen Testing: Various types of penetration tests exist, including:

7.5.5.1. Black Box Testing: Testers have no prior knowledge of the target system and attempt to find vulnerabilities as an external attacker would.

7.5.5.2. White Box Testing: Testers have full knowledge of the target system's architecture and code, often conducted by internal security teams.

7.5.5.3. Gray Box Testing: Testers have partial knowledge of the target system, simulating an attack by an insider with some privileged information.

7.5.5.4. Web Application Penetration Testing: Focused on web applications to identify vulnerabilities like SQL injection, cross-site scripting (XSS), and authentication flaws.

7.5.6. Key Activities: Penetration testing involves activities such as:

7.5.6.1. Identifying vulnerabilities through reconnaissance and scanning.

7.5.6.2. Attempting to exploit vulnerabilities to gain unauthorized access.

7.5.6.3. Reporting findings, including potential security risks and recommendations for remediation.

7.5.7. Benefits: Penetration testing offers several advantages:

7.5.7.1. Identifies vulnerabilities that may not be apparent through regular security assessments.

7.5.7.2. Mimics real-world attack scenarios, providing a practical assessment of security posture.

7.5.7.3. Helps organizations prioritize remediation efforts based on the severity of identified vulnerabilities.

7.5.7.4. Enhances security awareness and readiness to respond to incidents.

7.5.8. Differences Between Audits and Penetration Testing:

7.5.8.1. Purpose: Audits primarily focus on ensuring compliance and evaluating adherence to security policies, while penetration testing aims to uncover vulnerabilities and weaknesses by simulating cyberattacks.

7.5.8.2. Scope: Audits typically have a broader scope, encompassing policies, controls, and compliance, while penetration testing has a narrower focus on identifying specific vulnerabilities.

7.5.8.3. Approach: Audits are typically conducted as structured assessments, whereas penetration testing involves more dynamic and adversarial tactics to exploit vulnerabilities.

7.5.8.4. Timing: Audits are often scheduled at regular intervals, while penetration testing may be conducted periodically or in response to specific concerns or changes in the environment.

In summary, security audits and penetration testing are both vital components of a robust cybersecurity strategy. Audits help organizations assess their security posture and compliance, while penetration testing identifies vulnerabilities and weaknesses through simulated attacks. Together, these practices provide a comprehensive view of an organization's security readiness and help improve its overall security posture.

7.6. Key Components In Network Security And Their Associated Aspects

Network Security Component	Aspect/Function
Firewalls	• Packet filtering • Stateful inspection • Application layer filtering • Proxy services • Intrusion detection and prevention (IDS/IPS)
Intrusion Detection and Prevention (IDS/IPS)	• Signature-based detection • Anomaly-based detection • Real-time monitoring • Alerting and reporting
Antivirus/Antimalware	• Scanning for malware signatures • Heuristic analysis • Behaviour-based detection • Regular definition updates
VPN (Virtual Private Network)	• Encryption protocols (e.g., IPsec, SSL/TLS) • Authentication methods • Tunnelling and data confidentiality • Remote access control
Network Access Control (NAC)	• Identity and access

	management • Compliance checking • Guest network provisioning
Encryption	• Data encryption (at rest and in transit). • Secure key management. • Certificate management. • Secure communication protocols
Two-Factor Authentication (2FA)	• Token-based authentication. • Biometric authentication. • SMS or email verification. • Time-based one-time passwords (TOTP).
Web Application Firewall (WAF)	• Protection against OWASP Top Ten threats. • Signature-based filtering. • Behavioural analysis. • Logging and monitoring
Security Information and Event Management (SIEM)	• Log aggregation. • Correlation and analysis. • Incident detection and response.

	• Alerting and reporting.
Access Control	• User and group permissions • Role-based access control (RBAC). • Attribute-based access control (ABAC). • Centralized policy management.
Network Segmentation	• Isolation of network segments. • VLANs and Sub-netting. • Micro-segmentation. • Access control rules.
Mobile Device Management (MDM	• Device enrolment and provisioning. • Policy enforcement. • Remote wipe and lock. • Application whitelisting
Cloud Security	• Identity and access management. • Data encryption and key management. • Security monitoring and auditing.

- Compliance with cloud provider controls

Figure 4: Key components in network security and their associated aspects

Note: These components and aspects are essential elements of network security, but the implementation and configuration of each component can vary based on an organization's specific needs and the technology solutions they choose. Additionally, network security often involves a combination of these components working together to provide comprehensive protection against a range of threats.

Chapter 8: Data Protection and Encryption

8.1. Introduction

Data protection and encryption are fundamental aspects of cybersecurity that play a critical role in safeguarding sensitive information from unauthorized access, data breaches, and cyberattacks. Let's discuss these concepts in detail:

8.1.1 Data Protection: Data protection refers to the strategies, policies, and measures put in place to secure sensitive information and ensure its confidentiality, integrity, and availability.

Here are key aspects of data protection:

8.1.1.1 Data Classification: Organizations should classify data based on its sensitivity and importance. Common classifications include public, internal, confidential, and highly confidential. This helps in prioritizing protection efforts.

8.1.1.2 Access Control: Implement strict access controls to ensure that only authorized individuals or systems can access specific data. Access should be based on roles, responsibilities, and the principle of least privilege.

8.1.2 Data Lifecycle Management: Establish policies and procedures for the entire data lifecycle, including creation, storage, transmission, use, archiving, and disposal. This ensures data is handled securely throughout its existence.

8.1.3 Encryption: Encrypt data at rest and in transit to protect it from unauthorized access. Strong encryption algorithms and key management practices are essential components of data protection.

8.1.4 Data Backup and Recovery: Regularly back up critical data to prevent data loss due to hardware failures, cyberattacks, or other incidents. Develop and test data recovery plans to minimize downtime.

8.1.5 Data Loss Prevention (DLP): Implement DLP solutions to monitor and control the movement of sensitive data within and outside the organization. DLP helps prevent data leaks and unauthorized disclosures.

8.1.6 Security Awareness and Training: Educate employees about data protection policies, safe data handling practices, and how to recognize and report security incidents. Human error is a common cause of data breaches.

8.1.7 Incident Response: Develop a well-defined incident response plan that outlines procedures for detecting, responding to, and mitigating data breaches. Rapid response is crucial in minimizing the impact of a breach.

8.1.2 Encryption:

Encryption is a core security technique that transforms data into a format that is unreadable without the appropriate decryption key. It ensures data confidentiality and integrity and plays a crucial role in data protection:

8.1.2.1 Types of Encryption:

8.1.2.1.1 Symmetric Encryption: Uses a single shared key for both encryption and decryption. While efficient, securely managing and distributing the key is essential.

8.1.2.1.2 Asymmetric Encryption: Uses a pair of keys: a public key for encryption and a private key for decryption. This is commonly used in secure communication and digital signatures.

8.1.2.1.3 End-to-End Encryption: Ensures that data is encrypted on the sender's side, transmitted encrypted, and decrypted only by the intended recipient. Popular in secure messaging apps and online services.

8.1.2.1.4 Data at Rest Encryption: Encrypts data stored on devices, servers, or databases. Full-disk encryption and database encryption are examples.

8.1.2.1.5 Data in Transit Encryption: Secures data while it's being transmitted over networks, such as the internet. Transport Layer Security (TLS) and Secure Sockets Layer (SSL) are commonly used protocols for this purpose.

8.1.2.1.6 Key Management: Proper key management is essential for the effectiveness of encryption. Keys must be securely generated, stored, rotated, and revoked when necessary. Key management systems help automate these processes.

8.1.2.1.7 Secure Communication: Encryption ensures that data exchanged between clients and servers, or between devices, remains confidential. This is crucial for protecting sensitive information during online transactions, communication, and cloud storage.

8.1.2.1.8 Compliance and Regulations: Many industries and regions have specific data protection regulations that require encryption for certain types of sensitive data. For example, the Health Insurance Portability and Accountability Act (HIPAA) in healthcare and the General Data Protection Regulation (GDPR) in Europe have encryption requirements.

8.1.2.1.9 Open Source Encryption Tools: Open-source encryption libraries and tools, such as OpenSSL and GnuPG (GPG), provide accessible and transparent solutions for implementing encryption in various applications.

In summary, data protection and encryption are vital components of cybersecurity that help organizations safeguard sensitive information. They involve a combination of policies, technologies, and best practices to protect data throughout its lifecycle and ensure its confidentiality and integrity, whether at rest or in transit. Implementing strong data protection measures and encryption is essential for maintaining trust, complying with regulations, and mitigating the risks associated with data breaches.

8.2. Data Backup and Recovery

Data backup and recovery are critical components of a robust cybersecurity and business continuity strategy. They ensure that organizations can protect their data from loss or corruption and recover it in the event of a data breach, hardware failure, natural disaster, or other unexpected incidents. Here's a detailed discussion of data backup and recovery:

8.2.1 Data Backup:

8.2.1.1 Purpose of Data Backup: Data backup involves creating copies of data and storing them separately from the original to prevent data loss due to various factors like hardware failures, data corruption, cyberattacks, or accidental deletions.

8.2.2 Backup Types: There are several types of data backups, including:

8.2.2.1 Full Backup: Copies all data in a system or environment.

8.2.2.2 Incremental Backup: Backs up only the data that has changed since the last backup.

8.2.2.3 Differential Backup: Backs up data that has changed since the last full backup.

8.2.2.4 Snapshot Backup: Captures the state of data at a specific point in time.

8.2.2.5 Offsite Backup: Copies data to a remote location for disaster recovery.

8.2.3 Backup Frequency: The frequency of backups depends on the organization's data recovery objectives (Recovery Point Objective or RPO). Critical systems may require frequent backups (e.g., daily or hourly), while less critical data may be backed up less frequently.

8.2.4 Backup Methods: Organizations can use various backup methods, including tape backups, disk backups, cloud backups, and hybrid solutions. Cloud-based backups are becoming increasingly popular due to their scalability and ease of management.

8.2.5 Retention Policies: Establish data retention policies to determine how long backup copies should be kept. Compliance requirements and business needs influence these policies.

8.2.6 Data Recovery:

8.2.6.1 Purpose of Data Recovery: Data recovery is the process of restoring lost or compromised data to its original state or a usable form following an incident that caused data loss. The goal is to minimize downtime and data loss impact.

8.2.6.2 Recovery Points: Different recovery points can be chosen depending on the situation, such as:

8.2.6.3 Point-in-Time Recovery: Restoring data to a specific moment in time.

8.2.6.4 File-Level Recovery: Recovering individual files or folders.

8.2.7 Disaster Recovery: Recovering entire systems and data in case of catastrophic failures.

8.2.7.1 Recovery Time Objective (RTO): The RTO is the maximum acceptable downtime for a system or service. It determines how quickly data and systems need to be recovered after an incident.

8.2.7.2 Data Recovery Solutions: Data recovery solutions may include restoring data from backup copies, using redundant systems, or employing disaster recovery plans that involve failover to secondary data centres or cloud-based resources.

8.2.7.3 Testing and Validation: Regularly test data recovery procedures to ensure they work as expected. These tests help identify and address potential issues before a real disaster occurs.

8.2.7.4 Business Continuity and Disaster Recovery (BCDR): Data backup and recovery are integral components of BCDR plans. These plans encompass a broader strategy for ensuring business continuity in the face of disruptive events.

8.2.8 Best Practices for Data Backup and Recovery:

8.2.8.1 Automate Backups: Implement automated backup solutions to reduce the risk of human error and ensure backups occur regularly.

8.2.8.2 Offsite Backups: Store backup copies offsite to protect against on-site disasters like fires or floods.

8.2.8.3 Encryption: Encrypt backup data to safeguard it from unauthorized access, both during transmission and while at rest.

8.2.8.4 Regular Testing: Regularly test and validate data recovery procedures to ensure they are effective.

8.2.8.5 Documentation: Maintain clear and up-to-date documentation of backup and recovery processes.

8.2.8.6 Monitoring: Continuously monitor backup processes for failures or anomalies.

8.2.8.7 Access Controls: Implement access controls to restrict who can initiate backups and perform recoveries.

8.2.8.8 Incident Response: Integrate data recovery procedures into the organization's incident response plan to expedite recovery in the event of a breach or disaster.

In conclusion, data backup and recovery are essential for preserving data integrity and ensuring business continuity. A well-planned backup strategy, coupled with effective recovery procedures, helps organizations minimize the impact of data loss incidents and maintain operational resilience in the face of unexpected events.

8.3. Data Classification and Encryption

Data classification and encryption are integral components of data security and privacy strategies. They help organizations protect sensitive information, comply with data protection regulations, and mitigate the risks associated with data breaches. Here's a discussion of data classification and encryption, their importance, and how they work together:

8.3.1 Data Classification:

8.3.1.1 Purpose of Data Classification: Data classification is the process of protection required. The primary purpose is to identify and prioritize data protection efforts.

8.3.1.2 Classification Levels: Data is typically classified into several levels, such as:

- **Public Data:** Non-sensitive information that can be freely shared.
- **Internal Data:** Sensitive information for internal use only.
- **Confidential Data:** Highly sensitive data that requires strict access controls and protection.

- categorizing data based on its sensitivity, value, and the level of
    - **Restricted Data:** Data with the highest level of sensitivity, often subject to strict regulatory requirements.
        1. **Data Classification Criteria:** Criteria for classifying data may include its content, value, legal requirements, impact on the organization if compromised, and the potential harm to individuals if exposed.

2. **Data Classification Policies:** Establish data classification policies that specify how data should be categorized, handled, and protected. These policies guide employees in understanding the importance of data security.
3. **Access Control:** Data classification informs access control measures. Access should be granted based on the classification of the data, ensuring that only authorized individuals or systems can access sensitive information.

1. **Encryption:**
    1. **Purpose of Encryption: Encryption is the process of transforming data into a coded form to make it unreadable to unauthorized parties. The primary purpose is to ensure data confidentiality and protect it from interception or theft.**
    2. **Encryption Algorithms: Encryption uses algorithms and encryption keys to convert plaintext data into ciphertext. Common encryption algorithms include Advanced Encryption Standard (AES), RSA, and Elliptic Curve Cryptography (ECC).**
    3. **Data at Rest Encryption: Data at rest encryption involves encrypting data stored on devices, databases, or servers to protect it from physical theft or unauthorized access.**
    4. **Data in Transit Encryption: Data in**

transit encryption secures data as it is transmitted over networks. Protocols like Transport Layer Security (TLS) and Secure Sockets Layer (SSL) are commonly used for this purpose.

5. End-to-End Encryption (E2E): E2E encryption ensures that data is encrypted by the sender and decrypted only by the intended recipient, providing the highest level of data privacy.

2. How Data Classification and Encryption Work Together:
    1. Risk-Based Approach: Data classification helps organizations identify which data is sensitive and requires encryption. It guides the implementation of encryption measures based on the classification level.
    2. Access Control: Access to encrypted data is typically controlled based on the classification level. Only individuals or systems with the appropriate permissions should possess the decryption keys.
    3. Data Protection: Encryption provides an additional layer of protection for classified data. Even if unauthorized access occurs, encrypted data remains unreadable without the decryption keys.
    4. Compliance: Many data protection regulations, such as the General Data Protection Regulation (GDPR) and the Health Insurance Portability and Accountability Act (HIPAA),

recommend or require encryption for sensitive data. Proper data classification helps organizations identify which data falls under these regulations.

5. **Data Retention and Destruction: Data classification informs data retention and destruction policies. When data reaches the end of its lifecycle, proper disposal procedures must include secure data destruction methods, especially for highly classified data.**

In conclusion, data classification and encryption are essential components of a comprehensive data security strategy. Classification helps organizations understand the sensitivity of their data, while encryption provides a powerful means to protect it, ensuring confidentiality and compliance with data protection regulations. When implemented together, they create a robust defence against data breaches and unauthorized access.

8.4. Secure Data Handling Practices

Secure data handling practices are essential for safeguarding sensitive information and preventing data breaches. These practices involve a combination of policies, procedures, and security measures to ensure that data remains confidential, integral, and available only to authorized individuals or systems. Here are some key secure data handling practices:

8.4.1 **Data Classification:** Classify data based on its sensitivity, value, and the level of protection required. Common classifications include public, internal, confidential, and highly confidential.

8.4.2 **Access Control:** Implement strict access controls to ensure that only authorized individuals or systems can access specific data. Use mechanisms like role-based access control (RBAC) and least privilege access principles.

8.4.3. Encryption: Encrypt data at rest and in transit to protect it from unauthorized access. Ensure that encryption keys are securely managed, and use strong encryption algorithms.

8.4.4. Secure Data Storage: Store data securely, whether it's in databases, file systems, or cloud storage. Employ data loss prevention (DLP) solutions to monitor and control data movement.

8.4.5. Password Protection: Enforce strong password policies, including complex passwords and regular password changes. Implement multi-factor authentication (MFA) for added security.

8.4.6. Data Backup and Recovery: Regularly back up critical data to prevent data loss due to hardware failures or cyberattacks. Develop and test data recovery plans to minimize downtime.

8.4.7. Secure Data Transmission: Use secure protocols (e.g., HTTPS, SFTP) to transmit data over networks. Encrypt sensitive data during transmission to protect it from interception.

8.4.8. Employee Training: Educate employees about data protection policies, safe data handling practices, and how to recognize and report security incidents. Human error is a common cause of data breaches.

8.4.9. Data Retention and Destruction: Establish data retention policies that outline how long data should be kept and when it should be securely destroyed. Ensure proper disposal of physical and electronic data.

8.4.10. Logging and Monitoring: Implement comprehensive logging and monitoring of data access and activities. Regularly review logs for suspicious or unauthorized activities.

8.4.11. Incident Response: Develop a well-defined incident response plan that outlines procedures for detecting, responding to, and mitigating data breaches. Rapid response is crucial in minimizing the impact of a breach.

8.4.12. Vendor Security: If third-party vendors handle your data, ensure they have robust security practices in place. Assess their security measures and compliance with data protection regulations.

8.4.13. Compliance with Regulations: Ensure that data handling practices comply with relevant industry-specific regulations (e.g., GDPR, HIPAA, and PCI DSS) and data protection laws, where applicable.

8.4.14. Mobile Device Security: Implement mobile device management (MDM) solutions to secure smartphones and tablets used for work. Enforce encryption and remote wipe capabilities for lost or stolen devices.

8.4.15. Secure Development Practices: For software and application development, follow secure coding practices to prevent vulnerabilities that could expose sensitive data to exploitation.

8.4.16. Regular Security Audits and Testing: Conduct regular security assessments, including penetration testing and vulnerability scanning, to identify weaknesses in data handling practices and infrastructure.

8.4.17. Data Privacy Impact Assessment (DPIA): For privacy-sensitive projects, conduct DPIAs to assess the impact on data privacy and implement necessary measures to protect personal data.

8.4.18. Document Security: Secure physical and digital documents containing sensitive data. Use locked cabinets, access controls, and encryption for digital documents.

8.4.19. Cloud Security: If using cloud services, understand the shared responsibility model and ensure that data stored in the cloud is adequately protected through encryption and access controls.

8.4.20. Training and Awareness: Continuously educate and raise awareness among employees about the importance of data security and their role in protecting sensitive information.

Adhering to these secure data handling practices is crucial in today's digital age, where data is a valuable asset and data breaches can have severe consequences for individuals and organizations alike. A comprehensive approach to data security helps mitigate risks and maintain trust with customers and stakeholders.

Chapter 9: Incident Response and Disaster Recovery

9.1. Introduction:

Incident response and disaster recovery are two critical components of an organization's cybersecurity and business continuity strategy. They involve preparedness and actions taken to respond to and recover from unexpected events that can disrupt operations or compromise data security.

9.1.1 Incident Response:

9.1.1.1 Purpose: Incident response is a structured approach to addressing and managing security incidents, such as data breaches, cyberattacks, system compromises, and other security events. The primary purpose is to minimize the impact of incidents and swiftly return to normal operations.

9.1.1.2 Key Activities: Incident response involves several key activities:

- **Detection:** Detecting and identifying security incidents as soon as they occur.
- **Analysis:** Analysing the incident to understand its scope, nature, and potential impact.
- **Containment:** Taking immediate steps to limit the damage and prevent further spread of the incident.
- **Eradication:** Identifying and eliminating the root cause of the incident.
- **Recovery:** Restoring affected systems and services to normal operation.
- **Communication:** Effectively communicating with stakeholders, including employees, customers, and regulatory authorities.

- **Documentation:** Documenting the incident, actions taken, and lessons learned for future reference.
    1. **Incident Response Plan (IRP):** Organizations should have a well-documented incident response plan in place. This plan outlines roles and responsibilities, procedures, communication protocols, and steps to be followed in the event of a security incident.
    2. **Cybersecurity Tools:** Utilize cybersecurity tools like intrusion detection systems (IDS), security information and event management (SIEM) systems, and endpoint detection and response (EDR) solutions to aid in incident detection and response.
    3. **Incident Reporting:** Encourage a culture of incident reporting where employees and stakeholders promptly report any unusual or suspicious activities that could indicate a security incident.
    4. **Disaster Recovery:**
        1. **Purpose: Disaster recovery focuses on planning and implementing strategies to ensure the continuity of critical business operations and the recovery of IT systems and data in the event of a catastrophic event or disaster. These events can include natural disasters (e.g., hurricanes, earthquakes), infrastructure failures, or large-scale cyberattacks.**
        2. **Key Activities: Disaster recovery encompasses the following activities:**
    - **Risk Assessment:** Identifying potential threats and vulnerabilities that could lead to disasters.
    - **Business Impact Analysis (BIA):** Assessing the

impact of a disaster on critical business processes and systems.

- **Backup and Recovery:** Establishing processes for data backup, offsite storage, and rapid restoration of systems and data.
- **Testing and Training:** Regularly testing disaster recovery plans to ensure they are effective and training employees on their roles during a disaster.
- **Alternative Facilities:** Identifying alternative facilities or infrastructure that can be used in case of physical damage to primary locations.

1. **Disaster Recovery Plan (DRP):** Similar to an incident response plan, a disaster recovery plan is a comprehensive document that outlines procedures and processes for responding to disasters. It includes recovery time objectives (RTOs) and recovery point objectives (RPOs) for critical systems.
2. **Business Continuity:** Disaster recovery is closely related to business continuity planning, which includes broader strategies for maintaining essential business functions during and after a disaster. Business continuity plans often encompass both IT recovery and business process continuity.
3. **Cloud-Based Solutions:** Many organizations leverage cloud-based disaster recovery solutions, which provide scalability, redundancy, and data replication capabilities to ensure data and system availability even in the face of disasters.
4. **Key Differences:**

- **Focus:** Incident response focuses on managing and mitigating the impact of security incidents, while disaster recovery focuses on recovering IT systems and business operations after a disaster.

- **Triggers:** Incidents can result from various security events, while disasters are typically triggered by catastrophic events.
- **Scope:** Incident response often involves a more immediate and targeted response, while disaster recovery involves more extensive planning and preparation.

In summary, incident response and disaster recovery are essential components of an organization's ability to manage and recover from security incidents and unexpected disasters. Effective planning, preparation, and execution of these strategies help organizations minimize the impact of incidents and maintain business continuity even in challenging circumstances.

9.2. Developing an Incident Response Plan

Developing an incident response plan (IRP) is a crucial step in ensuring that your organization can effectively respond to and mitigate security incidents. A well-documented and well-structured IRP helps minimize the impact of incidents, protect sensitive data, and maintain business continuity. Here are the key steps to develop an incident response plan:

9.2.1. Establish an Incident Response Team: Identify and assemble a dedicated incident response team (IRT) consisting of individuals with the necessary skills and expertise. This team may include IT professionals, security experts, legal advisors, and public relations representatives.

9.2.2. **Define Incident Categories:** Categorize potential security incidents based on their severity and impact. Common categories include data breaches, malware infections, denial-of-service attacks, insider threats, and physical security incidents.

9.2.3. Create an Incident Response Policy: Develop a policy that outlines the organization's commitment to incident response and the key objectives of the IRP. This policy should be approved by senior management.

9.2.4. Conduct a Risk Assessment: Identify the critical assets, systems, and data within your organization. Conduct a risk assessment to understand the potential threats and vulnerabilities that could impact these assets.

9.2.5. Develop an IRP Document: Create a comprehensive incident response plan document that includes the following elements:

- **Roles and Responsibilities:** Define the roles and responsibilities of team members, including incident handlers, coordinators, and decision-makers.

- **Incident Identification:** Describe how incidents will be detected and reported within the organization.
- **Incident Classification:** Outline the criteria for categorizing incidents based on their severity.
- **Response Procedures:** Detail the steps to be taken in response to each type of incident, including containment, eradication, recovery, and lessons learned.
- **Communication Plan:** Define how internal and external communication will be handled during an incident, including who needs to be informed and when.
- **Legal and Compliance Considerations:** Address legal and regulatory requirements that may apply during incident response, such as data breach notification laws.
- **Training and Awareness:** Specify training requirements for incident response team members and general employee awareness programs.
- **Testing and Drills:** Describe how and when incident response plans will be tested through table-top exercises and full-scale drills.
- **Documentation and Reporting:** Explain the importance of documenting all actions taken during incident response and reporting to appropriate authorities, if necessary.

9.2.6. Incident Detection and Reporting: Implement mechanisms for detecting and reporting security incidents promptly. Encourage all employees to report suspicious activities or events that may indicate an incident.

9.2.7. Develop Communication Protocols: Establish communication protocols for notifying team members, executives, and external parties (such as law enforcement, regulatory bodies, and affected parties) when an incident occurs.

9.2.8. Testing and Training: Regularly conduct training sessions and table-top exercises to ensure that team members are familiar with the IRP and can respond effectively in a crisis.

9.2.9. Establish Relationships: Build relationships with external organizations and authorities that may be involved in incident response, such as law enforcement agencies and incident response teams from service providers.

9.2.10. Legal and Regulatory Compliance: Ensure that your IRP aligns with legal and regulatory requirements specific to your industry and geographic location.

9.2.11. Continuous Improvement: Periodically review and update the IRP to incorporate lessons learned from incidents, changes in technology, and evolving threats.

9.2.12. Incident Documentation: Document all actions taken during incident response, including containment, recovery, and investigation. This documentation is valuable for post-incident analysis and potential legal proceedings.

9.2.13. Reporting and Review: Report incidents to appropriate authorities, as required by law, and conduct a post-incident review to assess the effectiveness of the response and identify areas for improvement.

9.2.14. Public Relations Strategy: Develop a strategy for communicating with the media, customers, and stakeholders to protect the organization's reputation in the event of a significant incident.

9.2.15. Backup and Recovery: Ensure that backup and recovery procedures are integrated into the IRP to facilitate data restoration and system recovery.

9.2.16. Vendor and Third-Party Considerations: If third-party vendors handle your data or systems, ensure that their incident response capabilities align with your expectations and requirements.

Remember that an IRP is a living document that should be regularly reviewed, tested, and updated to address emerging threats and changes in your organization's environment. The goal is to be well-prepared to respond effectively to security incidents and minimize their impact on your organization's operations and reputation.

9.3. The Importance of Timely Detection and Response

The timely detection and response to security incidents are of paramount importance in the field of cybersecurity. This proactive approach is crucial for several reasons:

9.3.1. **Minimizing Damage:** Timely detection and response can significantly reduce the potential damage caused by security incidents. The quicker an incident is identified and contained, the less time it has to spread, steal data, disrupt operations, or cause harm.

9.3.2. **Preventing Data Breaches:** Rapid detection and response can prevent data breaches by stopping cybercriminals in their tracks. This is critical for safeguarding sensitive information, such as customer data, intellectual property, and financial records.

9.3.3. Reducing Downtime: Security incidents, especially malware infections or cyberattacks, can disrupt business operations. Timely response measures can help organizations recover systems and services faster, reducing downtime and minimizing financial losses.

9.3.4. Protecting Reputation: A swift and effective response can help organizations protect their reputation. Public perception of an organization can suffer if it is perceived as slow or ineffective in responding to security incidents.

9.3.5. Compliance with Regulations: Many data protection and cybersecurity regulations require organizations to report security incidents promptly and take action to mitigate them. Failing to do so can lead to legal and regulatory consequences.

9.3.6. Identifying Root Causes: Timely incident response allows organizations to investigate and identify the root causes of security incidents. This information is valuable for preventing future incidents and improving security measures.

9.3.7. Preventing Escalation: Some security incidents, if left unchecked, can escalate into larger and more damaging events. Timely detection and response can prevent this escalation.

9.3.8. Limiting Financial Impact: Security incidents can have significant financial implications, including costs associated with incident response, legal fees, fines, and potential litigation. Rapid containment and recovery efforts can help limit these financial burdens.

9.3.9. Maintaining Customer Trust: Timely incident response demonstrates an organization's commitment to protecting customer data and maintaining trust. A delayed or ineffective response can erode customer confidence.

9.3.10. Early Warning for Advanced Threats: Advanced and persistent threats often operate stealthily within an organization's systems. Timely detection allows organizations to identify these threats before they cause extensive damage.

9.3.11. Security Awareness and Training: Incidents provide valuable opportunities to raise security awareness among employees. Timely communication about incidents can reinforce the importance of security best practices.

9.3.12. Cyber Insurance Coverage: Some cyber insurance policies may require organizations to demonstrate a robust incident response capability to qualify for coverage. Timely detection and response are essential for meeting these requirements.

In summary, timely detection and response to security incidents are critical for minimizing damage, protecting data, maintaining business continuity, and preserving an organization's reputation. To achieve effective incident response, organizations should have well-documented incident response plans, trained response teams, and the necessary technologies and processes in place to detect and respond swiftly to security events. Proactive monitoring and continuous improvement of incident response capabilities are essential for staying ahead of evolving cybersecurity threats.

9.4. Creating a Disaster Recovery Plan

Creating a disaster recovery plan (DRP) is a crucial step in ensuring your organization's ability to recover and resume critical business operations in the event of a disaster or major disruption. An effective DRP helps minimize downtime, data loss, and financial losses. Here's a step-by-step guide to creating a disaster recovery plan:

9.4.1. Define Objectives and Scope: Clearly define the objectives of your disaster recovery plan, including recovery time objectives (RTOs) and recovery point objectives (RPOs). Determine the scope of the plan, which systems, applications, and data are critical, and what types of disasters or disruptions you are preparing for (e.g., natural disasters, cyberattacks, and hardware failures).

9.4.2. **Identify Critical Assets and Resources:** Identify the critical assets, systems, applications, and data that are essential for your organization's operations. Prioritize them based on their importance to your business.

9.4.3. Conduct a Risk Assessment: Perform a comprehensive risk assessment to identify potential threats and vulnerabilities that could lead to disasters or disruptions. This assessment should cover physical, technological, and operational risks.

9.4.4. Business Impact Analysis (BIA): Conduct a business impact analysis to assess the potential impact of a disaster on critical business processes and functions. This helps determine the order in which systems and processes need to be restored.

9.4.5. Develop the DRP Document: Create a detailed disaster recovery plan document that includes the following components:

- **Roles and Responsibilities:** Define the roles and responsibilities of individuals and teams involved in the recovery process.
- **Contact Information:** Maintain a list of contact information

for key personnel, vendors, and external agencies that may be involved in recovery efforts.

- **Recovery Procedures:** Document step-by-step procedures for recovering critical systems and applications. Include instructions for data restoration, hardware replacement, and software configuration.
- **Communication Plan:** Establish communication protocols for notifying team members, executives, and external parties in the event of a disaster.
- **Testing and Training:** Describe how and when disaster recovery plans will be tested through table-top exercises and full-scale drills. Ensure that team members are trained in their roles during recovery.
- **Documentation and Reporting:** Explain the importance of documenting all actions taken during disaster recovery and reporting to appropriate authorities if necessary.
- **Vendor and Supplier Relationships:** If third-party vendors or suppliers play a critical role in your operations, outline how you will work together in a disaster scenario.

9.4.6. Data Backup and Recovery: Implement robust data backup and recovery procedures, including regular backups, offsite storage, and methods for rapid data restoration. Ensure that backup and recovery solutions align with your RPO and RTO objectives.

9.4.7. Cloud-Based Solutions: Consider leveraging cloud-based disaster recovery solutions, which provide scalability, redundancy, and data replication capabilities, ensuring data and system availability even in the face of disasters.

9.4.8. Testing and Drills: Regularly test the disaster recovery plan through simulations and drills to ensure that it works effectively and that team members are familiar with their roles.

9.4.9. Document and Maintain Procedures: Maintain an up-to-date record of all recovery procedures, configurations, and contact information. Review and update the DRP document as needed to reflect changes in your organization's technology and operations.

9.4.10. Legal and Regulatory Compliance: Ensure that your DRP aligns with legal and regulatory requirements specific to your industry and geographic location, especially regarding data privacy and compliance.

9.4.11. Communication and Public Relations: Develop a strategy for communicating with the media, customers, and stakeholders to protect your organization's reputation in the event of a significant disaster.

9.4.12. Employee Awareness: Continuously educate employees about the importance of disaster recovery planning and their roles in the event of a disaster.

9.4.13. Continuous Improvement: Periodically review and update the disaster recovery plan to incorporate lessons learned from drills, changes in technology, and evolving threats.

9.4.14. Budget and Resources: Allocate the necessary budget and resources for the development, testing, and maintenance of the DRP.

9.4.15. Vendor and Third-Party Considerations: If third-party vendors or service providers are part of your disaster recovery strategy, ensure that their capabilities align with your objectives.

9.4.16. Compliance and Reporting: Ensure that your DRP includes provisions for complying with relevant regulatory requirements and reporting incidents as necessary.

In conclusion, a well-structured disaster recovery plan is essential for an organization's resilience in the face of unexpected disasters or disruptions. By following these steps and regularly reviewing and updating the plan, you can help ensure that your organization is prepared to recover and maintain critical business operations in challenging circumstances.

Chapter 10: Security Compliance and Regulations

10.1. Introduction:

Security compliance and regulations refer to the set of rules, standards, and legal requirements that organizations must adhere to in order to ensure the security, privacy, and protection of data and information assets. These regulations are established by governments, industry bodies, and regulatory authorities to mitigate risks, safeguard sensitive data, and maintain the integrity of various sectors, including healthcare, finance, and technology. Here's a more detailed definition of security compliance and regulations:

10.1.1 Security Compliance: Security compliance refers to an organization's adherence to specific security standards, guidelines, and best practices, whether mandated by laws and regulations or industry-specific requirements. It involves implementing security measures and controls to protect sensitive data, systems, and networks. Compliance efforts often include conducting security assessments, audits, and risk assessments to ensure that an organization meets the established security standards.

Key aspects of security compliance include:

1. **Legal and Regulatory Requirements:** Compliance with laws and regulations that pertain to data security, privacy, and information protection. Examples include the General Data Protection Regulation (GDPR), Health Insurance Portability and Accountability Act (HIPAA), and Payment Card Industry Data Security Standard (PCI DSS).
2. **Industry Standards:** Adherence to industry-specific security standards and frameworks, such as ISO 27001, NIST Cybersecurity Framework, and CIS Controls, which provide guidelines for safeguarding information.
3. **Internal Policies:** Development and enforcement of internal security policies and procedures that align with external

regulations and standards.

4. **Security Controls:** Implementation of security controls and measures, such as access controls, encryption, monitoring, and incident response plans, to protect data and systems.
5. **Auditing and Monitoring:** Ongoing monitoring and auditing of security controls to assess compliance and identify vulnerabilities or non-compliance issues.

10.1.2 Regulations: Regulations are legally binding directives issued by government authorities or regulatory bodies to govern specific aspects of security, data protection, and privacy within a given jurisdiction or industry. Regulations are designed to ensure that organizations handle sensitive information responsibly and securely and that individuals' privacy rights are protected.

Key examples of security and data protection regulations include:

1. **General Data Protection Regulation (GDPR):** Enforced in the European Union (EU), GDPR regulates the processing and protection of personal data and imposes strict requirements on organizations handling EU residents' data.
2. **Health Insurance Portability and Accountability Act (HIPAA):** Applies to the healthcare industry in the United States and sets standards for the secure handling of protected health information (PHI).
3. **Payment Card Industry Data Security Standard (PCI DSS):** Governs the security of credit card transactions and requires organizations that process payment card data to adhere to specific security controls.
4. **Sarbanes-Oxley Act (SOX):** Applies to publicly traded companies in the United States and focuses on financial reporting, but it also has implications for data security and controls.
5. **California Consumer Privacy Act (CCPA):** A state-level

regulation in California, USA that gives consumers more control over their personal data and requires certain data protection measures.

6. **Financial Industry Regulatory Authority (FINRA) Rules:** Imposes compliance requirements on firms in the financial industry to protect customer data and ensure market integrity.
7. **Federal Information Security Management Act (FISMA):** Applies to U.S. federal agencies and defines requirements for securing government information systems.
8. **Cybersecurity Maturity Model Certification (CMMC):** A U.S. Department of Defence regulation that mandates cybersecurity standards for contractors handling sensitive defence information.

Compliance with these regulations is legally mandated, and non-compliance can result in severe penalties, fines, legal actions, and reputational damage for organizations. Therefore, organizations often invest significant resources in ensuring they meet these requirements and maintain a strong commitment to data security and privacy.

10.2. GDPR, HIPAA, and Other Data Protection Laws

Several data protection laws and regulations exist worldwide to safeguard individuals' privacy and protect sensitive information. Two prominent ones are the General Data Protection Regulation (GDPR) and the Health Insurance Portability and Accountability Act (HIPAA). Let's explore these laws along with a few others:

10.2.1. General Data Protection Regulation (GDPR):

- **Jurisdiction:** European Union (EU) and European Economic Area (EEA)
- **Purpose:** GDPR aims to protect the privacy and personal data of EU/EEA residents. It imposes strict requirements on organizations that process personal data and grants individuals greater control over their data.
- **Key Provisions:** Consent, data subject rights (access, erasure, portability), data protection impact assessments (DPIAs), data breach notification, and appointment of data protection officers (DPOs).

10.2.2. Health Insurance Portability and Accountability Act (HIPAA):

- **Jurisdiction:** United States
- **Purpose:** HIPAA primarily governs the protection of healthcare data. It aims to ensure the confidentiality, integrity, and availability of electronic protected health information (ePHI) and regulates healthcare providers, health plans, and healthcare clearinghouses.
- **Key Provisions:** Privacy Rule (limits use and disclosure of

ePHI), Security Rule (establishes security standards), Breach Notification Rule (requires reporting of data breaches), and Omnibus Rule (strengthened HIPAA's privacy and security provisions).

10.2.3. California Consumer Privacy Act (CCPA):

- **Jurisdiction:** California, United States
- **Purpose:** CCPA grants California residents more control over their personal data held by businesses. It allows consumers to know what data is collected and shared and gives them the right to request its deletion.
- **Key Provisions:** Right to access, right to delete, right to opt-out of data sales, and restrictions on discrimination against consumers who exercise their rights.

10.2.4. Personal Data Protection Act (PDPA):

- **Jurisdiction:** Singapore
- **Purpose:** The PDPA governs the collection, use, and disclosure of personal data in Singapore. It aims to safeguard individuals' personal data while enabling organizations to use data for legitimate purposes.
- **Key Provisions:** Consent requirements, data protection provisions, and the establishment of a Data Protection Commission.

10.2.5. Privacy Act of 1974:

- **Jurisdiction:** United States (federal government)
- **Purpose:** The Privacy Act regulates the collection, use, and dissemination of personal information by U.S. federal

agencies. It grants individuals certain rights regarding their personal data held by federal agencies.

- **Key Provisions:** Access to personal records, the right to amend incorrect information, and limitations on disclosure of personal information without consent.

10.2.6. Personal Information Protection and Electronic Documents Act (PIPEDA):

- **Jurisdiction:** Canada
- **Purpose:** PIPEDA governs how private-sector organizations handle personal information. It balances the need for organizations to collect and use data with individuals' privacy rights.
- **Key Provisions:** Consent, access to personal information, and requirements for data protection.

10.2.7. Data Protection Directive:

- **Jurisdiction:** European Union (superseded by GDPR)
- **Purpose:** The Data Protection Directive (Directive 95/46/EC) was the predecessor to GDPR and established the framework for data protection in the EU. It influenced the development of GDPR.

These data protection laws vary in scope, jurisdiction, and requirements, but they all share the common goal of safeguarding personal data and ensuring individuals have some level of control over their information. Organizations that handle personal data must comply with the applicable laws and regulations in their jurisdiction to protect data privacy and avoid legal consequences.

10.3. Industry-Specific Regulations

In addition to general data protection and privacy regulations like GDPR and HIPAA, various industry-specific regulations and compliance requirements exist to address specific needs and challenges in various sectors. These regulations are tailored to the unique characteristics and risks associated with each industry.

Here are some examples of industry-specific regulations:

10.3.1 Financial Industry Regulations:

- **Sarbanes-Oxley Act (SOX):** Applies to publicly traded companies in the United States and focuses on financial reporting, but it also has implications for data security and controls.
- **Payment Card Industry Data Security Standard (PCI DSS):** Governs the security of credit card transactions and requires organizations that process payment card data to adhere to specific security controls.
- **Dodd-Frank Wall Street Reform and Consumer Protection Act:** Addresses financial regulatory reform and consumer protection in the United States, focusing on areas such as derivatives trading and risk management.

10.3.2. Healthcare Industry Regulations:

- **Health Insurance Portability and Accountability Act (HIPAA):** Protects the privacy and security of patient information in the healthcare industry, including electronic health records (EHRs).
- **HITECH Act:** The Health Information Technology for Economic and Clinical Health Act complements HIPAA by

focusing on the secure use and exchange of electronic health information.

- **Medical Device Regulation (MDR) and In-vitro Diagnostic Device Regulation (IVDR):** European regulations that ensure the safety and performance of medical devices and in-vitro diagnostic devices.

10.3.3. Energy and Utilities Regulations:

- **North American Electric Reliability Corporation Critical Infrastructure Protection (NERC CIP):** Governs the security of the North American power grid and requires utilities to implement security controls to protect critical infrastructure.

10.3.4. Telecommunications Regulations:

- **Communications Act of 1934:** Establishes the regulatory framework for telecommunications in the United States, including rules related to wiretapping and customer privacy.

10.3.5. Defence and Aerospace Regulations:

- **International Traffic in Arms Regulations (ITAR):** Regulates the export and import of defence-related articles and services to protect national security interests in the United States.
- **Defence Federal Acquisition Regulation Supplement (DFARS):** Contains cybersecurity requirements for contractors and subcontractors that work with the U.S. Department of Defence.

10.3.6. Pharmaceutical and Biotechnology Regulations:

- **Food and Drug Administration (FDA) Regulations:** FDA regulations cover the development, testing, and marketing of drugs and medical devices, including data security and privacy considerations.

10.3.7. Education Industry Regulations:

- **Family Educational Rights and Privacy Act (FERPA):** Protects the privacy of student education records and governs the release of such records in the United States.

10.3.8. Aviation Industry Regulations:

- **Federal Aviation Administration (FAA) Regulations:** Include requirements for the security of aviation infrastructure, data, and systems.

10.3.9. Environmental Regulations:

- **Environmental Protection Agency (EPA) Regulations:** Govern environmental data and reporting requirements for organizations in industries such as manufacturing and energy.

10.3.10. Food Safety Regulations:

- **Food Safety Modernization Act (FSMA):** Focuses on food safety regulations in the United States, including requirements for the security of food supply chains.

10.3.11. Gaming and Gambling Industry Regulations:

- **Gaming Control Act:** Varies by jurisdiction but typically regulates casinos, online gambling, and other gaming-related activities.

It's important for organizations operating in these industries to be aware of and comply with the specific regulations that apply to their sector. Non-compliance can result in legal penalties, fines, and reputational damage. Additionally, industry-specific regulations may evolve over time, so staying informed and keeping compliance efforts up to date is crucial.

10.4. Compliance Frameworks and Best Practices

Compliance frameworks and best practices provide organizations with guidelines, standards, and methodologies for achieving compliance with various regulations and ensuring the security and privacy of data. These frameworks offer a structured approach to address specific industry requirements and security challenges. Here are some key compliance frameworks and best practices:

10.4.1. National Institute of Standards and Technology (NIST) Frameworks:

- **NIST Cybersecurity Framework:** Developed by the U.S. NIST, this framework provides guidelines and best practices for managing and reducing cybersecurity risk. It consists of five core functions: Identify, Protect, Detect, Respond, and Recover.
- **NIST Risk Management Framework (RMF):** Designed for federal agencies, this framework outlines a structured process for managing information system security and compliance with the Federal Information Security Modernization Act (FISMA).

10.4.2. International Organization for Standardization (ISO) Standards:

- **ISO 27001:** Part of the ISO/IEC 27000 family, ISO 27001 is a globally recognized standard for information security management systems (ISMS). It provides a systematic approach for managing and protecting sensitive information.
- **ISO 22301:** This standard focuses on business continuity

management systems (BCMS) and helps organizations prepare for and respond to disruptions and disasters.

10.4.3. Payment Card Industry Data Security Standard (PCI DSS): Developed by the Payment Card Industry Security Standards Council (PCI SSC), PCI DSS sets requirements for securing payment card data. It applies to organizations that process, store, or transmit credit card information.

10.4.4. Health IT Standards and Regulations: Health IT Frameworks: Various frameworks and standards are used in the healthcare industry, such as Health Level Seven International (HL7) for healthcare data exchange and the Health Information Trust Alliance (HITRUST) Common Security Framework for healthcare risk management.

- **Electronic Health Record (EHR) Certification:** The Office of the National Coordinator for Health Information Technology (ONC) and the Certification Commission for Health Information Technology (CCHIT) provide certification programs for EHR systems.

10.4.5. Federal Information Security Management Act (FISMA): FISMA outlines information security requirements for federal agencies and provides guidelines for assessing and monitoring the security of federal information systems.

10.4.6. Centre for Internet Security (CIS) Controls: The CIS Controls are a set of best practices for improving an organization's cybersecurity posture. They provide prioritized actions that organizations can take to enhance security.

10.4.7. International Traffic in Arms Regulations (ITAR): ITAR regulations govern the export and import of defence-related articles and services. Compliance with ITAR is critical for organizations dealing with military or defence technologies.

10.4.8. Cloud Security Alliance (CSA) Best Practices: CSA offers guidelines and best practices for securing cloud computing environments. The CSA Security Trust Assurance and Risk (STAR) program provides a framework for cloud security assessments.

10.4.9. Data Protection Impact Assessment (DPIA): DPIA is a best practice recommended by the GDPR and other privacy regulations. It involves assessing the impact of data processing activities on individuals' privacy and implementing measures to mitigate risks.

10.4.10. Industry-Specific Guidelines: Many industries have their own sets of best practices and compliance guidelines, such as the Centre for Financial Professionals (CeFPro) for the finance sector and the Automotive Information Sharing and Analysis Centre (Auto-ISAC) for the automotive industry.

10.4.11. Regulatory Technology (RegTech) Solutions: RegTech companies offer technological solutions and platforms to help organizations automate compliance with various regulations, making it easier to manage and monitor compliance efforts.

Implementing these compliance frameworks and best practices can help organizations strengthen their security posture, protect sensitive data, and meet regulatory requirements. Organizations should choose the frameworks and practices that align with their specific industry, regulatory environment, and risk profile to ensure effective compliance and security.

Chapter 11: Cybersecurity for Small Businesses

11.1. Introduction

Cybersecurity is a critical concern for small businesses, just as it is for larger organizations. In fact, small businesses can be particularly vulnerable to cyberattacks due to limited resources and potentially less robust cybersecurity measures. Here are key considerations and strategies for implementing effective cybersecurity for small businesses:

11.1.1 Recognize the Importance of Cybersecurity: Small businesses must understand that they are not immune to cyber threats. Cyberattacks can result in data breaches, financial losses, and damage to reputation. Recognizing the significance of cybersecurity is the first step toward proactive protection.

11.1.2. **Conduct a Risk Assessment:** Identify and assess the specific cybersecurity risks that your small business faces. This includes evaluating the types of data you handle, potential vulnerabilities, and the likelihood and impact of various cyber threats.

11.1.3. Develop a Cybersecurity Policy: Create a clear and comprehensive cybersecurity policy that outlines security measures, acceptable use of technology, data protection protocols, and incident response procedures. Communicate this policy to all employees.

11.1.4. Employee Training and Awareness: Invest in cybersecurity training and awareness programs for your staff. Educate employees about common threats like phishing, social engineering, and malware. Encourage strong password practices and the use of multi-factor authentication.

11.1.5. Implement Strong Access Controls: Limit access to sensitive systems and data to only those employees who require it for their roles. Implement strong authentication methods and regularly review and update access permissions.

11.1.6. Regularly Update and Patch Software: Ensure that all software, including operating systems and applications, is up to date with the latest security patches and updates. Vulnerabilities in outdated software can be exploited by cybercriminals.

11.1.7. Secure Endpoints: Use endpoint security solutions, such as antivirus software and endpoint detection and response (EDR) tools, to protect computers and mobile devices from malware and other threats.

11.1.8. Data Encryption: Encrypt sensitive data, both in transit and at rest. Encryption helps protect data even if it falls into the wrong hands.

11.1.9. Back up Data: Regularly back up critical data to secure and offline locations. In the event of a ransomware attack or data loss, having backups can prevent data from being permanently lost.

11.1.10. Network Security: Use firewalls, intrusion detection and prevention systems, and network segmentation to protect your network from unauthorized access and attacks.

11.1.11. Incident Response Plan: Develop and document an incident response plan that outlines steps to take in case of a cybersecurity incident. This should include procedures for reporting incidents, containment, eradication, recovery, and communication with stakeholders.

11.1.12. Vendor Security: Assess the cybersecurity practices of third-party vendors and service providers, especially if they have access to your business's data or systems. Ensure they meet security standards.

11.1.13. Regular Security Audits: Conduct regular security audits and assessments to identify vulnerabilities and weaknesses in your cybersecurity posture. Consider engaging third-party security experts for thorough assessments.

11.1.14. Cyber Insurance: Consider purchasing cyber insurance to help mitigate the financial impact of a data breach or cyber incident.

11.1.15. Stay Informed: Keep up to date with the latest cybersecurity threats and trends. Subscribe to security news sources and participate in industry-specific cybersecurity forums and groups.

11.1.16. Compliance with Regulations: If your business deals with regulated data (e.g., payment card information, personal health data), ensure compliance with relevant industry-specific regulations (e.g., PCI DSS, HIPAA).

Remember that cybersecurity is an ongoing process, and threats evolve over time. Small businesses should prioritize a proactive and continuous approach to cybersecurity to protect their assets, maintain customer trust, and avoid costly data breaches.

11.2. Challenges Faced by Small Businesses

Small businesses face a range of challenges that can impact their operations, growth, and sustainability. Some of these challenges are common across various industries and sectors, while others are more industry-specific. Here are some of the key challenges faced by small businesses:

11.2.1. Limited Resources: Small businesses often operate with limited financial and human resources. This can make it challenging to invest in technology, hire specialized staff, and implement robust cybersecurity measures.

11.2.2 **Cybersecurity Threats:** Small businesses are increasingly targeted by cybercriminals due to perceived vulnerabilities. Cybersecurity threats, such as phishing, ransomware, and data breaches, can have a significant impact on small businesses with limited IT security resources.

11.2.3. Access to Capital: Securing financing and access to capital can be a major hurdle for small businesses, particularly start-ups. Limited funding can restrict growth opportunities, hinder product development, and affect day-to-day operations.

11.2.4. Competition: Small businesses often compete with larger, more established competitors. Competing with companies that have greater resources and market presence can be challenging.

11.2.5. Regulatory Compliance: Small businesses must navigate various regulations, licenses, and permits at the local, state, and federal levels. Ensuring compliance with these requirements can be complex and time-consuming.

11.2.6. Hiring and Retaining Talent: Attracting and retaining skilled employees can be difficult, especially when competing with larger firms that may offer better compensation and benefits packages.

11.2.7. Marketing and Branding: Small businesses may struggle to effectively market their products or services and establish a strong brand presence in a crowded marketplace.

11.2.8. Cash Flow Management: Maintaining a healthy cash flow is crucial for small businesses. Managing expenses, invoicing, and ensuring timely payments can be challenging.

11.2.9. Technology Adoption: Staying up to date with technology and incorporating it into business operations can be a significant challenge. Small businesses may lack the resources for technology investments and training.

11.2.10. Economic Volatility: Economic downturns, market fluctuations, and unexpected events (e.g., pandemics) can disproportionately affect small businesses, making it difficult to plan for the future.

11.2.11. Supply Chain Disruptions: Small businesses that rely on complex supply chains may face disruptions due to factors such as natural disasters, trade disputes, or global events.

11.2.12. Scaling and Growth: Achieving sustainable growth while maintaining profitability can be a delicate balancing act for small businesses. Rapid growth can strain resources and lead to operational challenges.

11.2.13. Health and Safety Compliance: Meeting health and safety regulations, especially during public health crises, can be a significant challenge, requiring adaptations and additional investments.

11.2.14. Customer Retention: Building and retaining a loyal customer base can be challenging. Small businesses must consistently deliver value and excellent customer service to keep customers coming back.

11.2.15. Access to Markets: Expanding into new markets or reaching a broader customer base can be difficult for small businesses, particularly those with limited distribution channels.

Navigating these challenges requires resilience, adaptability, strategic planning, and sometimes seeking external support, such as business mentoring, grants, or partnerships. Small businesses that effectively address these challenges can increase their chances of success and long-term sustainability.

11.3. Budget-Friendly Security Measures

Small businesses with limited budgets can still implement effective security measures to protect their digital assets and data. Here are some budget-friendly security measures that can help enhance cybersecurity:

11.3.1. Employee Training and Awareness: Invest in cybersecurity training and awareness programs for employees. Educate them about phishing, social engineering, and safe online practices. Creating a security-conscious culture can be one of the most cost-effective measures.

11.3.1. **Strong Password Policies:** Implement and enforce strong password policies. Encourage employees to use complex passwords and consider implementing multi-factor authentication (MFA) wherever possible, which is often provided by free or low-cost authentication apps.

11.3.3. Regular Software Updates: Ensure that all software, including operating systems and applications, is kept up to date with the latest security patches and updates. Enabling automatic updates can simplify this process.

11.3.4. Firewall and Antivirus Software: Use free or low-cost firewall and antivirus software to protect endpoints and network traffic. Many reliable options are available at no cost.

11.3.5. Secure WI-Fi Networks: Secure your Wi-Fi networks with strong passwords, WPA3 encryption, and a separate guest network. Regularly change default router passwords.

11.3.6. Data Encryption: Enable encryption for sensitive data, both in transit and at rest. Many operating systems and applications offer built-in encryption features.

11.3.7. Regular Backups: Implement regular data backups to secure and offline storage. Affordable cloud backup services are available, and using them can protect against data loss due to ransomware or hardware failures.

11.3.8. Employee Access Control: Limit employee access to only the systems and data necessary for their roles. This can help minimize the risk of insider threats.

11.3.9. Mobile Device Security: Enforce security policies for mobile devices used by employees. This may include requiring passcodes, enabling remote wipe capabilities, and using mobile device management (MDM) tools.

11.3.10. Open-Source Security Tools: Explore open-source security tools and solutions that can provide cost-effective cybersecurity capabilities. Examples include Snort (network intrusion detection system) and OSSEC (host-based intrusion detection system).

11.3.11. Security Audits and Vulnerability Scanning: Regularly conduct security audits and vulnerability scanning using free or low-cost tools. These assessments can help identify weaknesses that need attention.

11.3.12. Cloud-Based Security Services: Consider cloud-based security services, such as cloud-based email filtering, web application firewalls (WAFs), and endpoint protection, which can be more affordable and scalable than traditional on-premises solutions.

11.3.13. Vendor Security Assessment: When working with third-party vendors or service providers, assess their security practices and ensure they meet your security standards. This can help protect your business from supply chain vulnerabilities.

11.3.14. Incident Response Plan: Develop an incident response plan to outline the steps to take in the event of a security incident. Preparedness can save time and resources during an incident.

11.3.15. Security Forums and Information Sharing: Engage with online security forums and communities to stay informed about emerging threats and best practices. Sharing knowledge with peers can be invaluable.

While these budget-friendly security measures can enhance cybersecurity, it's essential to assess your specific risks and compliance requirements to tailor your security strategy accordingly. Prioritizing security, even with limited resources, is a prudent investment to protect your business from potential cyber threats.

11.4. Outsourcing Security Services

Outsourcing security services is a strategic approach that many organizations, including small businesses, take to enhance their cybersecurity posture. This practice involves partnering with third-party security providers or Managed Security Service Providers (MSSPs) to manage various aspects of cybersecurity.

Here are key considerations and benefits of outsourcing security services:

11.4.1. Expertise and Specialization: Security service providers are experts in cybersecurity. They have specialized knowledge, experience, and resources to address complex security challenges, which may be beyond the capabilities of in-house teams.

11.4.2 **Cost-Effective Solutions:** Outsourcing can be cost-effective compared to hiring and maintaining an in-house security team with salaries, benefits, and ongoing training costs. You can tailor services to your budget and needs.

11.4.3. 24/7 Monitoring and Response: MSSPs offer around-the-clock monitoring and threat detection, ensuring rapid response to security incidents, even during non-business hours.

11.4.4. Scalability: You can scale security services up or down based on your organization's evolving needs. This scalability is particularly beneficial for growing businesses.

11.4.5. Access to Advanced Tools and Technologies: Security service providers often have access to cutting-edge cybersecurity tools and technologies that may be expensive for small businesses to acquire and maintain.

11.4.6. Compliance and Regulatory Assistance: MSSPs can help ensure that your organization complies with industry-specific regulations and standards, such as GDPR, HIPAA, or PCI DSS.

11.4.7. Focus on Core Business Activities: Outsourcing security services allows your team to concentrate on core business functions rather than being burdened with managing security operations.

11.4.8. Rapid Incident Response: MSSPs can quickly respond to security incidents, minimizing damage and reducing downtime.

11.4.9. Threat Intelligence and Analysis: Providers often have access to threat intelligence feeds and can analyse emerging threats, providing proactive protection.

11.4.10. Reduced Recruitment and Retention Challenges: Finding and retaining skilled cybersecurity professionals can be difficult. Outsourcing eliminates these recruitment challenges.

11.4.11. Risk Mitigation: MSSPs can help mitigate security risks by identifying vulnerabilities and implementing necessary controls.

11.4.12. Vendor and Supply Chain Security: Service providers can assess the security practices of third-party vendors and suppliers, reducing supply chain vulnerabilities.

11.4.13. Business Continuity and Disaster Recovery: MSSPs can help develop and manage business continuity and disaster recovery plans to ensure operational resilience.

11.4.14. Customized Solutions: Security providers can tailor their services to meet your organization's unique security needs and objectives.

11.4.15. Regular Reporting and Metrics: Providers typically offer regular reports and metrics to track the effectiveness of security measures and demonstrate compliance to stakeholders.

Despite these advantages, outsourcing security services does require careful consideration:

1. Vendor Selection: Choose a reputable and trustworthy security service provider with a proven track record and experience in your industry.

2. **Service-Level Agreements (SLAs):** Define clear SLAs to ensure that the provider meets your expectations regarding response times, reporting, and incident handling.

3. **Data Privacy and Confidentiality:** Ensure that the provider has robust data protection measures in place to safeguard your sensitive information.

4. **Continuous Communication:** Maintain open communication with your security service provider to address evolving threats and security needs.

5. **Cost Analysis:** Carefully assess the cost-benefit of outsourcing versus maintaining an in-house security team or other security solutions.

Outsourcing security services can be a strategic and cost-effective way for organizations, including small businesses, to enhance their cybersecurity defences and focus on their core operations while leveraging the expertise of specialized providers. However, it's essential to conduct thorough due diligence when selecting a provider and to maintain active oversight of your security program.

Chapter 12: Looking Ahead: Future Trends in Cybersecurity

12.1. Introduction

The field of cybersecurity is constantly evolving as cyber threats become more sophisticated and technology advances. Staying ahead of these trends is crucial for organizations to protect their digital assets and data. Here are some future trends and developments in cybersecurity:

12.1.1 Artificial Intelligence (AI) and Machine Learning (ML): AI and ML are being used by both cybercriminals and cybersecurity professionals. AI can automate threat detection, analyse vast datasets for anomalies, and enhance security incident response. On the flip side, cybercriminals may leverage AI to craft more convincing phishing emails and launch automated attacks.

12.1.2. **Zero Trust Security:** Zero Trust is an approach that assumes no trust, even within a network perimeter. It requires continuous verification of users and devices, regardless of their location, before granting access to resources. This model is gaining traction to combat insider threats and reduce the attack surface.

12.1.3. Extended Detection and Response (XDR): XDR solutions integrate and correlate data from multiple security sources (e.g., endpoint, network, and cloud) to provide a more comprehensive view of threats. They offer improved threat detection and response capabilities compared to traditional security information and event management (SIEM) systems.

12.1.4. Cloud Security Posture Management (CSPM): As organizations increasingly adopt cloud services, CSPM tools are becoming essential. They help ensure that cloud configurations are secure, compliant, and free from misconfigurations that could expose data to risks.

12.1.5. Quantum Computing and Post-Quantum Cryptography: The advent of quantum computing presents both opportunities and threats to cybersecurity. While quantum computing can break some traditional encryption algorithms, it also opens the door to new forms of quantum-resistant encryption and security protocols.

12.1.6. Threat Intelligence Sharing: Collaboration and sharing threat intelligence among organizations, industry sectors, and government agencies are becoming more critical to identify and mitigate emerging threats effectively.

12.1.7. 5G Security: The rollout of 5G networks brings faster speeds but also introduces new security challenges. It's essential to address issues like network slicing, IoT device security, and potential vulnerabilities in 5G infrastructure.

12.1.8. Internet of Things (IoT) Security: The growing number of IoT devices increases the attack surface for cybercriminals. Organizations will need to invest in IoT security solutions and best practices to protect their networks and data.

12.1.9. Biometric Authentication: Biometrics, such as fingerprint and facial recognition, are becoming more prevalent in authentication. However, ensuring the security and privacy of biometric data is a critical concern.

12.1.10. Supply Chain Security: Cyberattacks targeting the software supply chain have increased. Organizations will need to implement robust supply chain security practices and perform thorough vendor risk assessments.

12.1.11. Regulatory Evolution: Privacy and data protection regulations like GDPR and CCPA will likely continue to evolve, imposing stricter requirements on organizations worldwide. Compliance will remain a top priority.

12.1.12. Human-Centric Security: Recognizing that humans are often the weakest link in cybersecurity, organizations will focus on training and awareness programs to empower employees to recognize and respond to threats effectively.

12.1.13. Resilience and Incident Response: Preparing for and responding to cyber incidents will continue to be a priority. Organizations will invest in incident response plans, cyber insurance, and cyber resilience strategies.

12.1.14. AI-Driven Threats: Cybercriminals may increasingly use AI to automate attacks, personalize phishing attempts, and evade traditional security measures. Defenders will need to counter AI-driven threats with AI-driven defences.

12.1.15. Ethical Hacking and Bug Bounty Programs: Organizations will expand their use of ethical hackers and bug bounty programs to identify vulnerabilities and weaknesses before malicious actors can exploit them.

To stay ahead in the ever-evolving landscape of cybersecurity, organizations must adopt a proactive, adaptive, and holistic approach to security. This involves continuous education, threat intelligence sharing, investment in advanced technologies, and a strong focus on both prevention and incident response. Cybersecurity is an ongoing process, and vigilance is key to mitigating emerging threats effectively.

12.2. Artificial Intelligence and Machine Learning in Cybersecurity

Artificial Intelligence (AI) and Machine Learning (ML) are playing increasingly crucial roles in cybersecurity by enhancing threat detection, incident response, and overall security posture. Here's how AI and ML are being leveraged in cybersecurity:

12.2.1. Threat Detection and Prevention:

- **Anomaly Detection:** AI/ML can analyse vast amounts of data and identify unusual patterns or behaviours that may indicate a cyber threat. This can include abnormal network traffic, unusual user behaviour, or deviations in system activity.
- **Predictive Analytics:** Machine learning algorithms can predict potential security threats based on historical data and patterns. This allows organizations to proactively address vulnerabilities before they are exploited.
- **Signatureless Detection:** Traditional signature-based antivirus and intrusion detection systems rely on known patterns of attacks. ML-based systems can identify previously unseen threats by analysing behaviour and attributes, reducing reliance on signatures.

12.2.2. Malware Detection and Prevention:

- **Behaviour-Based Detection:** ML models can analyse the behaviour of files and processes in real-time to identify malicious activity. This is particularly effective against polymorphic malware that frequently changes its code.
- **Sandboxing and Isolation:** AI-powered sandboxes can execute suspicious files in a controlled environment to observe

their behaviour and determine if they are malicious.

12.2.3. Email Security:

- **Spam and Phishing Detection:** AI can analyse email content, sender behaviour, and metadata to identify phishing emails and spam. ML models can learn from past data to improve accuracy over time.
- **Natural Language Processing (NLP):** NLP algorithms can help identify social engineering attempts and malicious content within emails.

12.2.4. User and Entity Behaviour Analytics (UEBA): ML can establish a baseline of normal user behaviour and detect anomalies that may indicate insider threats or compromised accounts. UEBA tools help identify unusual patterns, such as excessive data access or unauthorized login attempts.

12.2.5. Network Security:

- **Intrusion Detection and Prevention:** ML can enhance network intrusion detection systems (NIDS) by identifying suspicious network traffic patterns and known attack signatures.
- **Network Segmentation:** AI can help automate network segmentation to contain and isolate threats quickly.

12.2.6. Endpoint Security:

- **Endpoint Detection and Response (EDR):** EDR solutions use ML to monitor and analyse endpoint activities in real-time, detect threats, and respond to incidents.
- **Behavioural Analysis:** ML models on endpoints can monitor

and detect unusual behaviour, such as file modifications or registry changes, indicative of malware or intrusions.

12.2.7. Security Automation and Orchestration: AI and ML can automate routine security tasks, freeing up cybersecurity teams to focus on more complex threats. Security orchestration platforms can use AI to streamline incident response workflows.

12.2.8. Deception Technologies: AI-driven deception technologies create fake assets within a network to attract and divert attackers. Machine learning helps make these decoys appear convincing and detect attacker interactions.

12.2.9. Threat Intelligence: AI can analyse large volumes of threat intelligence data from various sources to identify emerging threats and prioritize potential risks.

12.2.10. Fraud Detection: In the financial sector, ML models are used to detect fraudulent transactions by identifying unusual spending patterns and behaviour.

While AI and ML offer significant advantages in cybersecurity, it's essential to be aware of potential limitations, such as the risk of adversarial attacks against ML models and the need for ongoing model training and monitoring. Additionally, AI and ML should complement, not replace, human expertise in cybersecurity, as human judgment and contextual understanding remain critical in decision-making and incident response.

12.3. Quantum Computing and Its Impact on Encryption

Quantum computing has the potential to revolutionize computing by solving complex problems at speeds that classical computers cannot achieve. While this offers various opportunities for scientific research and optimization, it also poses a significant challenge to traditional encryption methods. Here's how quantum computing may impact encryption:

12.3.1. Breaking Existing Encryption Algorithms: Quantum computers have the potential to break widely used encryption algorithms, such as RSA and ECC (Elliptic Curve Cryptography), by exploiting their vulnerabilities to quantum attacks. Shor's algorithm, for example, can efficiently factor large numbers, which is the basis for breaking RSA encryption.

12.3.2. Impact on Data Confidentiality: If quantum computers can break existing encryption algorithms, data that was previously considered secure may become vulnerable to unauthorized access. This could have profound implications for data confidentiality in various sectors, including finance, healthcare, and government.

12.3.3. Need for Post-Quantum Cryptography (PQC): The advent of quantum computing has prompted the development of post-quantum cryptography (PQC) algorithms. These cryptographic methods are designed to be secure against quantum attacks. Examples of PQC algorithms include lattice-based cryptography, hash-based cryptography, and code-based cryptography.

12.3.4. Transition Period: Transitioning from classical encryption to PQC is a complex and gradual process that will take time. Organizations must plan for this transition to ensure the long-term security of their data.

12.3.5. Quantum Key Distribution (QKD): Quantum computing also offers potential solutions to the security challenges it poses. Quantum Key Distribution (QKD) is a technology that leverages the principles of quantum mechanics to secure communication channels. QKD can provide theoretically unbreakable encryption keys.

12.3.6. Hybrid Encryption: A practical approach is to adopt hybrid encryption schemes that combine classical encryption with PQC or QKD. This approach maintains security even in the presence of quantum threats.

12.3.7. Research and Development: Quantum-resistant encryption is an active area of research and development. Cryptographers are working to identify and develop encryption methods that will remain secure in the era of quantum computing.

12.3.8. Regulatory and Compliance Considerations: Organizations operating in regulated industries, such as finance and healthcare, must monitor the evolving regulatory landscape and ensure that they remain compliant with encryption requirements in the context of quantum computing.

12.3.9. Quantum-Safe Cryptographic Standards: Standardization bodies, such as NIST (National Institute of Standards and Technology), are actively working on establishing quantum-safe cryptographic standards to guide the adoption of PQC methods.

12.3.10. Quantum-Safe Solutions for Blockchain and Cryptocurrencies: The blockchain and cryptocurrency industries are exploring quantum-resistant cryptographic solutions to protect digital assets and transactions from quantum attacks.

In summary, quantum computing has the potential to disrupt classical encryption methods, and organizations need to prepare for the transition to quantum-resistant encryption techniques. This transition will require careful planning, investment in research and development, and cooperation among industry stakeholders to ensure the security of data and communications in a post-quantum world.

12.4. Biometric Authentication and Identity Management

Biometric authentication and identity management are technologies and processes that leverage unique physical or behavioural traits of individuals to verify their identities. These methods have gained popularity due to their convenience and high level of security. Here's an overview of biometric authentication and identity management:

12.4.1 Biometric Authentication: Biometric authentication involves verifying a person's identity based on their unique biological or behavioural characteristics. Common biometric traits used for authentication include:

1. **Fingerprint Recognition:** Scanning and matching the unique patterns of ridges and valleys on a person's fingertip.
2. **Facial Recognition:** Analysing the unique features of a person's face, such as the distance between their eyes or the shape of their nose and mouth.
3. **Iris Recognition:** Scanning the unique patterns in a person's iris, the coloured part of the eye.
4. **Voice Recognition:** Analysing the unique vocal characteristics and speech patterns of an individual.
5. **Retina Recognition:** Scanning the unique patterns of blood vessels in the back of the eye.
6. **Hand Geometry:** Analysing the size and shape of a person's hand, including the length and width of fingers.
7. **Behavioural Biometrics:** This includes the analysis of unique behavioural traits, such as typing patterns (keystroke dynamics), gait analysis, and signature recognition.

12.4.2 Identity Management: Identity management refers to the processes and technologies used to establish, maintain, and verify the identities of individuals within an organization or system. Key components of identity management include:

1. **User Provisioning:** The process of creating and managing user accounts, including assigning roles and permissions.
2. **Authentication:** Verifying the identity of users when they attempt to access systems or data. This may involve single sign-on (SSO), multi-factor authentication (MFA), or biometric authentication.
3. **Authorization:** Determining what resources and data users are allowed to access based on their roles and permissions.
4. **Identity Lifecycle Management:** Managing user identities throughout their entire lifecycle, from onboarding to offboarding.
5. **Access Control:** Enforcing policies that govern who has access to what resources, ensuring data security and compliance.
6. **Password Management:** Implementing password policies, including complexity requirements and password reset procedures.
7. **Audit and Logging:** Monitoring user activities and maintaining logs for security and compliance purposes.

12.4.3. Benefits of Biometric Authentication and Identity Management:

- **Security:** Biometric authentication offers a high level of security because it is based on unique, difficult-to-replicate traits.
- **Convenience:** Biometric authentication methods are convenient for users as they don't require remembering passwords or carrying physical tokens.

- **Reduced Fraud:** Biometrics can help reduce fraud and identity theft since it is challenging for an imposter to replicate biometric traits.
- **Efficiency:** Identity management systems streamline user provisioning and de-provisioning, reducing administrative overhead.
- **Compliance:** Effective identity management helps organizations meet regulatory compliance requirements by controlling access and auditing user activities.

12.4.4. Challenges and Considerations:

- **Privacy:** Storing and using biometric data must be done with utmost care to protect individuals' privacy.
- **False Positives and Negatives:** Biometric systems may have errors, leading to false acceptances (allowing unauthorized users) or false rejections (denying authorized users).
- **Spoofing:** Biometric systems can be vulnerable to spoofing attacks using fake biometric samples (e.g., fingerprints or faces).
- **Cost:** Implementing biometric authentication and identity management systems can be expensive, requiring specialized hardware and software.
- **Regulatory Compliance:** Organizations must ensure they comply with relevant data protection and privacy regulations when collecting and storing biometric data.

Biometric authentication and identity management offer significant advantages in terms of security and convenience but require careful planning, implementation, and consideration of privacy and regulatory concerns. They are widely used in various industries, including finance, healthcare, government, and technology.

Conclusion

The Ongoing Battle against Cyber Threats

The battle against cyber threats is an ongoing and ever-evolving challenge for individuals, businesses, governments, and organizations worldwide. Cyber threats continue to increase in sophistication, frequency, and impact. Here are key aspects of the ongoing battle against cyber threats:

1. **Evolving Threat Landscape:** Cyber threats are constantly evolving. Cybercriminals and threat actors adapt to security measures, develop new attack techniques, and exploit emerging technologies and vulnerabilities.

2. **Advanced Persistent Threats (APTs):** APTs are long-term, targeted cyberattacks typically associated with nation-states or well-funded hacking groups. They require continuous vigilance and sophisticated defences to detect and mitigate.

3. **Ransomware Attacks:** Ransomware attacks have become increasingly prevalent and damaging. These attacks encrypt victims' data and demand ransom payments for decryption keys.

4. **Phishing and Social Engineering:** Phishing attacks and social engineering techniques remain highly effective, often exploiting human vulnerabilities to gain unauthorized access or steal sensitive information.

5. **Insider Threats:** Insider threats, whether intentional or unintentional, pose a significant risk to organizations. Monitoring and managing insider threats require a combination of technology and human intervention.

6. **Cybersecurity Skills Gap:** There is a shortage of skilled cybersecurity professionals to defend against cyber threats. Organizations struggle to find and retain qualified cybersecurity experts.

7. Zero-Day Vulnerabilities: Zero-day vulnerabilities are software vulnerabilities unknown to the vendor. Attackers can exploit these vulnerabilities before patches are available, making proactive defences critical.

8. State-Sponsored Attacks: Nation-states engage in cyber espionage, cyber warfare, and cyberattacks against other countries, further complicating the cybersecurity landscape.

9. Regulatory Changes: Governments worldwide are enacting new regulations and data protection laws, such as GDPR and CCPA, which impose strict cybersecurity requirements and reporting obligations on organizations.

10. Cloud Security: As organizations migrate to the cloud, securing cloud infrastructure and data becomes paramount. Misconfigurations and cloud-specific threats are emerging concerns.

11. Internet of Things (IoT) Security: The proliferation of IoT devices introduces new attack surfaces. Insecure IoT devices can be compromised and used as entry points into networks.

12. Supply Chain Risks: Cyberattacks targeting the supply chain can disrupt operations and compromise the security of products and services.

13. International Collaboration: The global nature of cyber threats necessitates international collaboration between governments, law enforcement agencies, and private-sector organizations to combat cybercrime effectively.

14. Threat Intelligence Sharing: Organizations share threat intelligence to stay informed about emerging threats. Information sharing helps build a collective defence against cyber threats.

15. Security Automation and AI: Security automation and artificial intelligence are used to enhance threat detection, response, and incident investigation.

16. Cybersecurity Awareness: Ongoing cybersecurity awareness and training for employees are essential to prevent human errors and vulnerabilities.

17. Incident Response Planning: Developing and testing incident response plans is crucial to minimize the impact of cyberattacks and ensure a swift recovery.

18. Continuous Monitoring: Continuous monitoring of network traffic, endpoints, and systems helps detect and respond to threats in real-time.

19. Red Teaming and Penetration Testing: Organizations conduct red teaming and penetration testing exercises to proactively identify vulnerabilities and weaknesses.

20. Ethical Hacking and Bug Bounty Programs: Organizations engage ethical hackers and run bug bounty programs to find and address vulnerabilities before malicious actors can exploit them.

The battle against cyber threats is relentless, requiring a multi-faceted approach that combines technology, processes, skilled professionals, and a commitment to continuous improvement. It is a collective effort involving individuals, organizations, governments, and the cybersecurity industry to stay one step ahead of evolving threats.

The Role of Every Individual in Cybersecurity

Cybersecurity is not solely the responsibility of IT professionals or security experts. Every individual within an organization, as well as individuals in their personal lives, plays a crucial role in maintaining a secure digital environment. Here are key aspects of the role of every individual in cybersecurity:

1. **Security Awareness:** Stay informed about the latest cybersecurity threats and best practices. Awareness is the first line of defence against cyberattacks.
2. **Password Hygiene:** Create strong, unique passwords for all online accounts and change them regularly. Consider using a password manager to keep track of passwords.
3. **Multi-Factor Authentication (MFA):** Enable MFA wherever possible to add an extra layer of security to your accounts. This can prevent unauthorized access even if your password is compromised.
4. **Phishing Awareness:** Be cautious of unsolicited emails, messages, or calls. Verify the authenticity of requests for personal or financial information, especially when they come from unknown sources.
5. **Social Engineering Awareness:** Recognize common social engineering tactics, such as impersonation, pretexting, and baiting. Be sceptical of requests for sensitive information.
6. **Safe Web Browsing:** Avoid visiting suspicious or untrusted websites. Be cautious when downloading files or clicking on links, especially from unknown sources.
7. **Software Updates:** Keep your operating system, applications, and antivirus software up to date with the latest security patches. Many cyberattacks target known vulnerabilities.

8. Mobile Device Security: Secure your smartphones and tablets with passcodes or biometric authentication. Download apps only from trusted sources.

9. Safe File Sharing: Exercise caution when sharing files or documents, especially sensitive information. Use secure methods and encryption when necessary.

10. Data Backup: Regularly back up important data to secure and offline storage. This can protect against data loss due to ransomware or hardware failures.

11. Privacy Protection: Review privacy settings on social media platforms and limit the information you share online. Be aware of the data collected by apps and services.

12. Home Network Security: Secure your home Wi-Fi network with a strong password and encryption. Change default router passwords and update firmware regularly.

13. Avoid Public Wi-Fi Risks: Exercise caution when using public Wi-Fi networks, as they may not be secure. Use a virtual private network (VPN) when connecting to public Wi-Fi.

14. Reporting Security Incidents: If you suspect a security incident at work or in your personal life, report it to the appropriate authorities or IT/security teams.

15. Education and Training: Participate in cybersecurity training and awareness programs provided by your organization. Continuously improve your knowledge and skills.

16. Encourage a Culture of Security: Promote cybersecurity awareness within your organization or community. Encourage colleagues, friends, and family members to follow best practices.

17. Personal Device Security: Apply the same cybersecurity principles to personal devices, such as laptops, tablets, and smartphones, as you do to work devices.

18. Responsible Email Practices: Avoid forwarding chain emails or spam messages. Use the "Reply All" option judiciously to prevent email overload.

19. Limit Access: Limit access to your personal and professional information only to those who need it. Be cautious about sharing sensitive data.

20. Encourage Safe Habits in Others: - Encourage family members, friends, and colleagues to practice good cybersecurity habits and share resources to help them stay safe online.

The role of every individual in cybersecurity is vital because cyber threats often target human vulnerabilities. By being vigilant, educated, and proactive, individuals can contribute significantly to the overall security posture of their organizations and communities. Cybersecurity is a shared responsibility, and everyone has a part to play in protecting digital assets and data.

References:

1. *Chen, Thomas; Robert, Jean-Marc (2004). "The Evolution of Viruses and Worms"[1]. Archived from the original[2] on 2009-05-17. Retrieved 12 June, 2023.*
2. *Fred Cohen (1983-11-03). "Computer Viruses – Theory and Experiments"[3]. eecs.umich.edu. Retrieved 13 June 2023.*
3. *Mukosha, Patrick (2023), Fortifying Digital Fortress: A Comprehensive Guide to Information Systems Security, ISBN 9798223335160,*
4. *Mukosha, Patrick (2023), Unravelling Information Systems: Exploring the Core Concepts, ISBN 9798223630845*
5. *Szor, Peter (2005). The Art of Computer Virus Research and Defense[4]. Symantec Press[5] / Addison-Wesley[6] Professional. ISBN[7] 978-0-321-30454-4[8].*
6. *"Freddy Virus"[9], Virus Information Summary List, December 1992. Retrieved 12 August 2023.*
7. *"Magistr - the Virus Encyclopedia"[10]. The Virus Encyclopedia. Retrieved 14 March 2023.*
8. *Kimmo (March 3, 2008). "MBR Rootkit, A New Breed of"[11]. F-Secure. Retrieved 2023-03-01.*

---

1. *https://web.archive.org/web/20090517083356/http:/vx.netlux.org/lib/atc01.html*

2. *http://vx.netlux.org/lib/atc01.html*

3. *http://www.eecs.umich.edu/~aprakash/eecs588/handouts/cohen-viruses.html*

4. *https://books.google.com/books?id=XE-ddYF6uhYC&pg=PT204*

5. *https://en.wikipedia.org/wiki/Symantec_Press*

6. *https://en.wikipedia.org/wiki/Addison-Wesley*

7. *https://en.wikipedia.org/wiki/ISBN_(identifier)*

8. *https://en.wikipedia.org/wiki/Special:BookSources/978-0-321-30454-4*

9. *http://wiw.org/~meta/vsum/view.php?vir=529*

10. *http://virus.wikidot.com/magistr*

11. *http://www.f-secure.com/weblog/archives/00001393.html*

9. *"sKyWIper: A Complex Malware for Targeted Attacks"[12] (PDF). Budapest University of Technology and Economics[13]. 28 May 2012. Archived from the original[14] (PDF) on 28 May 2012. Retrieved 21 May 2023.*
10. *"NGRBot"[15], Enigma Software Group, 15 October 2012. Retrieved 4 March, 2023.*
11. *Goodin, Dan (2013-11-27). "New Linux worm targets routers, cameras, "Internet of things" devices"[16]. Ars Technica[17]. Retrieved March 8, 2023.*
12. *Sterling, Bruce (2014-01-29). "Linux.Darlloz, the Internet-of-Things worm"[18]. Wired[19]. Retrieved 24 August 2023.*

---

12. *https://web.archive.org/web/20120528142705/http:/www.crysys.hu/skywiper/skywiper.pdf*

13. *https://en.wikipedia.org/wiki/Budapest_University_of_Technology_and_Economics*

14. *http://www.crysys.hu/skywiper/skywiper.pdf*

15. *http://www.enigmasoftware.com/ngrbot-removal/*

16. *https://arstechnica.com/security/2013/11/new-linux-worm-targets-routers-cameras-internet-of-things-devices/*

17. *https://en.wikipedia.org/wiki/Ars_Technica*

18. *https://www.wired.com/2014/01/spime-watch-linux-darlloz-internet-things-worm/*

19. *https://en.wikipedia.org/wiki/Wired_(magazine)*

Did you love *"Computer Viruses Unveiled: Types, Trends and Mitigation Strategies"*? Then you should read *"Exploring Computer Systems: From Fundamentals to Advanced Concepts"*[20] by Patrick Mukosha!

[21]

The essential manual "Exploring Computer Systems: From Fundamentals to Advanced Concepts" takes readers on a thorough tour of the world of computer systems. This book offers a thorough examination of computer systems, starting with the fundamentals and advancing to complex concepts.

The book's excellent basis in computer architecture and components at the outset makes it understandable for both newcomers and seasoned IT experts. The basic concepts of hardware, software, and

20. https://books2read.com/u/bzBBxG

21. https://books2read.com/u/bzBBxG

their relationships are covered, enabling readers to comprehend how contemporary computer systems operate within.

Readers delve into the complexities of operating systems, including as process management, memory management, and file systems, as they move through the chapters. The author is succinct and straightforward. These complicated subjects are demystified by the author's succinct and simple explanations, making them understandable to readers of all skill levels.

This book's covering on networking and communication protocols is one of its best qualities. It offers a thorough review of computer networking and communication in local and wide-area networks, illuminating terms like TCP/IP, routing, and security. The fascinating worlds of virtualization and cloud computing are also highlighted in the book. The impact of virtual machines and cloud services, which have transformed the IT environment and increased computing flexibility, scalability, and affordability, is explained to readers.

About the Author

Patrick Mukosha is a Management Consultant originally from Kitwe, Copperbelt Province of Zambia. He has a Doctorate in Management (Strategic Management) and Masters (Strategic Planning) from Atlantic International University, USA. He also holds a bachelor's in Information Technology from University of East Anglia, Norwich, UK, and a Diploma in Business Management from Canterbury College of Technology, Canterbury, UK. Member of the Institute for Leadership Development, York University, USA (2001–08), He was elected Vice President-Midlands of Computer Society of Zambia (2004), Executive Director for VISION-2011 – a consortium of NGOs (2009 – 2011, Founder of Strategic Management Community of Zambia (2017), Vice Chairperson Mungule Ward Development Committee (2021-2026). He has worked for more than 15 years for International IT and Telecommunication companies in senior management portfolios. After finishing his PhD in 2017, he embarked on career as a Management Consultant. He has worked on several Strategic Planning projects and conducts coaching and mentorship in Entrepreneurship, Business Management, Strategic Management and ICT. He's an aggressive serial entrepreneur and founder of PatWest Technologies.

www.ingramcontent.com/pod-product-compliance
Lightning Source LLC
LaVergne TN
LVHW101613210926
848480LV00008B/364

* 9 7 9 8 2 2 3 6 9 2 7 9 9 *